S

*Presented To*

_____

*By*

_____

*On This Date*

_____

S

# HOLINESS
## *in* HIDDEN
# PLACES

## JONI
## EARECKSON
## TADA

COUNTRYMAN®

Published by J. Countryman, a Division of Thomas Nelson, Inc., Nashville, Tennessee 37214.

Project Editor—Terri Gibbs
Special Assistants—Francie Lorey, Kim Scherrei

Designed by Left Coast Design Inc., Portland, Oregon,

ISBN: 08499-5367-7

Printed and bound in the United States of America

*For Bob Flaig . . . and for Carol,*

*who's looking forward to seeing him again*

*Foreword* 6

## BEFORE YOU BEGIN...

To be holy means to be separated, set apart for God.

We have an instinct for holiness. That is, if we've experienced the new birth. This instinct, when first planted in our heart, is faint, gentle and tender, like the wisp of a grain of mustard seed. An instinct must grow, and so we learn about holiness through experience just as the Lord Jesus did when He *"learned obedience from what he suffered"* (Heb. 5:8).

Living more than thirty years as a quadriplegic, I'm acquainted with the "suffering" part. It's the "learning" I'm still working on. I learn not only from God's Word, but from watching others. I've met people in the oddest places who have served as an example of holiness to me. You'll meet some of them in this book. I've watched them drastically obey. I've seen them survive tough, cramped choices to become shining examples of the Master who learned obedience from what He suffered. I'm not imitating the holiness of these people, just how they got there!

I want to "get there," too. I'm learning to love this rugged life of being set apart for God. My soul stirs, and I feel courage rise when I choose to follow God in the small decisions, the stop-and-start successes, as well as the failures. Yes, the path to holiness is painful and at times unpleasant, but its pleasures and rewards are matchless and utterly superior. My wheelchair has shown me that the path of holiness is not an easy journey . . . but it's the right—no, the righteous—one.

In this book, you will read about holiness where you least expect it: in the most unlikely people and in the most hidden places. You will find it in humility. You will even see glimpses of it in glory. It's my prayer that as your instinct grows into a holy habit, as you strive to be like the Savior, you will learn obedience from the things you suffer. You will become the shining example.

And you'll discover holiness in the hidden places of your life.

**Joni Eareckson Tada**
*Spring 1999*

# HOLINESS...

# WHERE
# YOU LEAST
# EXPECT IT

# A NARROW ESCAPE

It was night time. Topanga Canyon Boulevard was at its busiest. Right under a dark overpass, my handicap-equipped van conked out. Everything went dead: the engine, the lights, and, to my horror, the brakes and steering. I was careening up a busy boulevard without any controls. I yanked violently on the braking mechanism, but my puny shoulder muscles were no match for the weight of a three-quarter-ton van rolling forward.

I was able to put a lid on my panic when the van finally drifted to a stop just short of the next intersection. Cars kept speeding around me.

After most of the traffic moved through the intersection, just when I thought I was safe, I screamed—my van was drifting backward! *Oh, God, help me, help me!* I whimpered as I strained with all my might to pull back on the brake. I glanced in the rearview mirror and saw the headlights of oncoming traffic barreling up the boulevard. The van continued to drift in reverse. In the dark. With no tail lights. I braced myself for the sound of screeching brakes and a rear-end collision.

*Is this the way I'm going to die? In a fiery crash? God, have You abandoned me?*

Just as I quit struggling and hunched over, waiting for a rear-end crash, I spotted Ken's truck. I knew he'd been driving somewhere behind me, but I didn't expect him to be the first to reach me out of the pack of traffic.

He screeched to a halt. As cars zoomed by, he jumped out of his truck, bolted into the van, and manhandled the

braking mechanism to a stop. Ken lifted me out of my wheelchair and carried me to his truck—all this while horns honked and drivers kept flicking their high beams. Never before had we been in such danger.

Weeks later, my nerves are still rattled. And when I lay my head on the pillow at night, images of "what could have happened" jar me awake.

Something else bothers me: my vulnerability. I've always leaned hard on God's protection for "the helpless," but in my most helpless moment, when I could do absolutely nothing for myself, what happed to my trust in Him?

> *He who dwells in the shelter of the Most High will rest in the shadow of the Almighty.*
>
> **PSALM 91:1**

My confidence in God isn't as unshakable as I thought. It hurts to know that my faith is so fragile. When I read "The Lord is my light and my salvation—whom shall I fear?" (Ps. 27:1), my answer is "I fear dead batteries and no brakes." That's why, to shore up my faith, I've been re-reading a few biblical accounts of the way God helps His people. I keep coming back to the story of Jesus calming the storm.

I have to admit I used to scoff at the disciples being so afraid. *What's the big deal about a storm?* I used to think. *So what if their boat nearly capsized. Good grief, they had Jesus right there with them, even if He was asleep.*

I'm not so cocky anymore. Now when I read the account in Luke, I notice words like, "the boat was being swamped" and "they were in great danger." There's no soft-pedaling it. The narrow escape out of that storm was a horrifying experience for each of them. Their fear was real, and their lack of trust in God understandable.

Like the disciples, I, too, was in great danger, with my vehicle about to capsize. I, too, was within inches of death. Fear seized me, just as it did them.

But I take comfort in this: although it seemed like God was asleep when I was at the wheel, He wasn't. He was there. I remind myself that no matter if it's by the skin of the teeth or with miles to spare . . . God helps His people. If it's not their appointed time to die, God will deliver them.

God will keep us. He'll help. He'll intervene—perhaps just in the nick of time. Is that too close for comfort? Maybe. But our trust in Him was never meant to be comfortable—only close.

And the nick of time *is* close enough.

LOS ANGELES, CALIF. (AP)—*Expensive video equipment used by pornographers was damaged when an earthquake hit January 17, 1994 in the San Fernando Valley. Severe damage occurred where an estimated 80% of the nation's sex-oriented videos are produced, most within five miles of the earthquake's epicenter.*

Lots of us who live in the San Fernando Valley smiled when we read that. Was God's hand of judgment slapping the City of Angels? Or should I say, City of *Fallen* Angels?

Some Christians in LA were quick to heap on fire and brimstone, reminding friends and neighbors of God's old reward-and-punishment way of dealing with sin-sick men. But underscore the word *old* because I, for one, am relieved that LA is not getting what it deserves. Back at the cross God put into motion a new way of dealing with sin-sick humans— even pornographers.

When lightning bolts hit or AIDS spreads or mudslides swamp a city, it sure looks like judgment. It feels like judgment. The fact is, God no longer deals with us in judgment but in mercy. If people got what they deserved, this old planet would have ripped apart at the seams centuries ago. Praise God that because of His great love "we are not consumed, for his

13

compassions never fail" (Lam. 3:22). He still has compassion on this wretched, sin-stained planet. His mercies, which are new every morning, assure us that we can live on one more day of God-borrowed time.

That's why, while Ken cleaned up the glass and splintered wood around our house after the earthquake, I sat in our backyard and sang out over the San Fernando Valley, "Our God is an awesome God, He reigns over heaven above in wisdom, power, and love . . . our God is an awesome God!"

*Awesome?* Yes. *Powerful?* You bet. Full of love and compassion? Always. So why does He allow earthquakes and floods and freezes?

The disciples asked the same sobering question when a tower fell on eighteen of their neighbors. Jesus knew they were thinking about reward-and-punishment when He explained, "Those eighteen who died when the tower in Siloam fell on them—do you think they were more guilty than all the others living in Jerusalem? I tell you, no! But unless you repent, you too will all perish" (Luke 13:4-5). Jesus was reminding them that natural disasters are not so much judgments as wake-up calls to repent. They are early warning signals.

Because of God's great love, towers, for the most part, stay put. A devastating flood happens only once every 500 years. Tornados miss most trailer parks. Hurricanes peter out by the time they reach New York City. And an earthquake erupts at 4:31 A.M. on a holiday morning when freeways are empty. Truly, God is merciful! God is faithful!

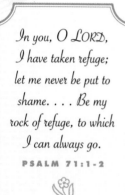

*In you, O LORD, I have taken refuge; let me never be put to shame. . . . Be my rock of refuge, to which I can always go.*

PSALM 71:1-2

It's a few weeks till summer, but already the corn is growing tall and green, stalks rustling in the breeze. A field of ripening corn is a glorious sight on a fine sunny day. I rediscovered this recently as Ken and I drove along a straight country road from St. Louis to Chicago.

At the beginning of our journey I glanced out the window and remarked, "Look at that beautiful cornfield, Ken . . . why, it stretches for as far as the eye can see." Fifty miles later, and at least double that number of farms, the long road and the fields of corn seemed to go on forever. After a hundred miles of endless cornfields, I shook my head and exclaimed, "We've been on this road for ages. Look around us—who in the world eats all this corn?"

It's odd how I failed to look on the bright side. Instead of thinking, *Isn't it wonderful that our country can feed itself and so many others on such plenty*, I thought, *How boring . . . this long road and all this corn.*

It happens whenever we find ourselves on an interminable, straight stretch in the same direction. No matter if it's a road, a two-hour lecture, or a line that snakes for blocks, it's hard not to become weary. To keep your mind awake, your senses sharp. It's also easy to ignore, or even forget, all the good fruit and rich grain that's being produced along the way.

Someone once said that the challenge of living is to develop *a long obedience in the same direction*. When it's demanded, we can rise on occasion and be patient . . . as long as there are limits. But we balk when patience is required over a long haul. We don't much like endurance.

It's painful to persevere through a marriage that's forever struggling. A church that never crests 100 members. Housekeeping routines that never vary from week-to-week. Even caring for an elderly parent or a handicapped child can feel like a long obedience in the same direction.

If only we could open our spiritual eyes to see the fields of grain we're planting, growing, and reaping along the way. That's what happens when we endure. Even the three decades I've lived in a wheelchair is, in a way, like driving on a long, straight road through miles and miles of cornfields—I have to keep reminding myself of the harvest of righteousness being produced in my life. "No discipline seems pleasant at the time, . . . later on, however, it produces a harvest of righteousness and peace for those who have been trained by it" (Heb. 12:11).

Right now you may be in the middle of a long stretch of the same old routine. The beginning of your Christian life was exhilarating. Your spiritual adrenaline was pumped up. But now there are miles behind you and miles to go. You don't hear any cheers or applause. The days run together— and so do the weeks. Your commitment to keep putting one foot in front of the other is starting to falter.

Take a moment and look at the fruit. *Perseverance. Determination. Fortitude. Patience.*

Your life is not a boring stretch of highway. It's a straight line to heaven. And just look at the fields ripening along the way. Look at the tenacity and endurance. Look at the grains of righteousness. You'll have quite a crop at harvest . . . so don't give up!

Let us not become
weary in doing good,
for at the proper time
we will reap a harvest
if we do not give up.

GALATIANS 6:9

# WE CAN LAUGH...NOW

"Did we see God work miracles on this trip, or *what!*" I smiled to Judy as we boarded our plane home. It had been a grand weekend of ministry, reminding me once again of the joy of serving Jesus.

Then our plane landed. It hadn't been the best of flights, but we were glad to be back. Then we sat curbside at the airport, our smiles fading as we kept checking our watches—

the handicap *Super Shuttle* never did turn up. After an hour of heat, car fumes, yelling cops, and honking horns, Judy hailed a cab, jammed in our luggage, and enlisted the reluctant cab driver's help to transfer me into the front seat. We chugged away from the curb and— clunk! The engine died.

Our driver abandoned us to find help, while impatient motorists screeched by shaking their fists. Judy tried to squirm past the luggage in the back seat to open my passenger door, but she was stuck. We were helpless to do anything but wait.

After a police officer jump-started the cab, we proceeded up the San Diego freeway, crawling at twenty-five miles per hour. It was rush hour. "Whaat eez dis terrible traffick!" our Iranian cab driver yelled, waving his hand in disgust. I eyed the ticker chocking up miles . . . and money.

> *Holiness is inwrought by the Holy Spirit, not because we have suffered, but because we have surrendered.*
>
> **RICHARD SHELLEY TAYLOR**

An hour and a half later, we pulled up to my driveway. How I longed for Ken to be home to greet us, but he was away fishing. I missed him. And I missed him even more when Judy realized that, between us, we didn't have enough cash for the enormous cab fare. "No checks, lady," our driver shook his head. "No credit cards, either."

Judy hurried to the front door, turned the key, and— brrrring!—the house alarm went off. I had given her the wrong code! Exasperated, she fumbled with the alarm buttons, opened the door, and let me in. I assured her I'd be okay by myself until she came back—the cab driver had to take her to Ralph's Market so she could cash a check to pay him.

My nerves were raw, my back was aching, and I was exhausted from the three-hour time change. As I began to power my wheelchair through the house, suddenly—brrrring!—I had tripped the motion sensor. When I wheeled to the control panel to try to punch the off button, I burst into tears: my paralyzed hands could only flop against the panel, striking even more buttons. My head was pounding . . . but . . . it wasn't my head . . . it was the front door—Judy had failed to abort the silent alarm to the police station. It was the Calabasas cops. "I'm sorry," I screamed above the alarm, "I can't open the door!" They replied, but I couldn't hear them—the telephone was ringing.

Finally Judy returned. The cops left and the cab left. She slumped against the front door . . . and we cried. No, we laughed. Then we cried some more. "Well, it *was* a great ministry weekend," we consoled each other, at which point we started laughing again.

I shouldn't be surprised at trials like these, especially on the heels of a fantastic ministry trip. I'd like to describe kaput engines and tripped alarms as tricks of the devil, but in fact they are simply a dead engine and a perfectly-working house alarm. It's part of the territory that comes with serving Jesus. Christian service includes the ordinary, earthly challenges.

If we're going to stand up and make a difference for Christ, while others lounge about, you can be sure we'll encounter hardships, obstacles, nuisances, hassles, and inconveniences—much more than the average couch potato. And we shouldn't be surprised. Such difficulty while serving Christ isn't necessarily suffering—it's status quo.

# CLOSE TO THEE

Thou my everlasting portion
More than friend or life to me,
All along my pilgrim journey,
Savior, let me walk with Thee.

chorus:
Close to Thee, close to Thee,
Close to Thee, close to Thee,
All along my pilgrim journey,
Savior, let me walk with Thee.

Not for ease or worldly pleasure,
Nor for fame my prayer shall be;
Gladly will I toil and suffer,
Only let me walk with Thee.

Lead me through the vale of shadows,
Bear me o'er life's fitful sea;
Then the gate of life eternal
May I enter, Lord, with Thee.

*Lyrics: Fanny J. Crosby, 1874*
*Music: Silas J. Vail, 1874*

# POLITICALLY
# CORRECT SINNERS

eople and labels. They really don't go together. It's much nicer just to push aside the politically correct protocol, snip off the label, and look at each other as . . . people.

I tried this during a luncheon with some inner-city pastors from Chicago. I wheeled up to the discussion table set with notepads and pencils. My goal was to learn about the unique needs of disabled people living in the city. The pastors, from some of the liveliest, most community-concerned churches in Chicago, were anxious to discuss how they could best minister to families with a disabled child.

As I talked with the pastors I wondered to myself. *Am I supposed to say African-American as I talk to these men? Or would they prefer Black? I know the word "colored" is out . . . although it's okay to say "people of color." So which is it? Black or African-American?*

I thought about my husband, Ken, who is of Japanese descent. His mother prefers the word *Oriental* while he prefers *Asian*. But his dad liked the term *Japanese-American*.

I shelved my thoughts and stuck to the topic of disabilities. The subject of color didn't come up.

Later on when the topic of Hispanic churches was discussed, I got tongue-tied between Hispanic and Latino. I decided then to ask the pastors how they wished to be addressed, whether as Black or African-American. They looked at each other, slapped the table, and laughed out loud. They had been wrestling with some questions, too.

During lunch, they had watched me being fed a sandwich by my friend and wondered, *Now when we refer to her, are we supposed to say "handicapped"? Or "physically challenged"? We know we're not supposed to refer to her as a cripple or an invalid . . . but what is correct?*

"All during lunch we were itching to know how you wanted to be called . . . you know, all those fancy terms," they said. "We didn't want to say the wrong thing and were wondering what was right!"

So what did we conclude? Labels don't matter. The important thing is to remember the person's name.

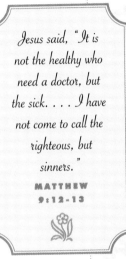

*Jesus said, "It is not the healthy who need a doctor, but the sick. . . . I have not come to call the righteous, but sinners."*
**MATTHEW 9:12-13**

True, some terms pass with age such as the word *colored* or the word *crippled*. Over time, such words change in meaning as language evolves. They drop by the wayside, weighted down by negative stereotypes. That's why a few of these pastors preferred *African-American*. It's why I prefer the word *disabled* over a term like *handicapped*. It's a matter of prudence—knowing what's appropriate in a given situation. But what is *always* appropriate is the person's name!

Labels, labels, labels. I'm glad Jesus referred to people as people. He never mentioned His friend being a coward, He simply called him Peter. He never referred to the woman who loved Him deeply as a prostitute, He just called her Mary Magdalene.

Jesus loved people. I'm sure that's why He often used their names when talking to them. "Peter, Peter . . ." He says at a moment of confrontation and forgiveness. "Martha, Martha . . ." He says at a moment of advice and counsel.

If there's any label at all, Jesus chooses one like "dear friends" or "little children" or "my brothers."

Or "sinners."

That may be the only label that fits, because it fits us all. Red or yellow, black or white, standing or sitting, blind or with sight. We're all sinners in need of a Savior—it's one label I don't mind wearing.

ush here, rush there . . . My friend Judy was steering me in my wheelchair through thick Christmas crowds at the mall. Much to our dismay the chair's batteries had just died. Judy was huffin' and puffin' past the shoppers as she pushed, then halted short of someone's shins. Finally, she panted, "I can't push this heavy thing anymore. What if I park you by Crabtree & Evelyn while I go pick up our packages?"

"No problem," I nodded. She disappeared into the crowd of shoppers while I waited. In the midst of pandemonium, I did what I always do. I waited and sat still. Very still.

It's a fact of life. Because I'm paralyzed from the shoulders down, a large part of me never moves. I don't run, I sit. I don't race, I wait. My body is in constant repose. My upright, sitting-straight position is never changing. Even when my wheels are tracking miles beneath me, I stay put. I can be scurrying through a jam-packed schedule, doing this and that, but a big part of me—due to my paralysis—is always quiet. Always tranquil.

That's why, if you'd seen me sitting by Crabtree & Evelyn, you would have noticed a satisfied smile. I was thanking God for my built-in stillness. Looking around at my harried and harrassed co-shoppers, I could appreciate my plight.

But it hasn't always been that way. My "natural" stillness used to drive me crazy. After my diving injury, I laid still for three months waiting to be moved from the intensive care unit into a regular hospital room. After more months of lying still,

I was finally moved to a rehabilitation center. While in rehab, I stayed put in my wheelchair for hours outside of physical therapy, waiting my turn to go in. And in the evenings, my manufactured stillness would madden me as I sat by the door waiting for friends or family to come for a visit.

It was more frightening when I laid down at night. In bed, gravity became my enemy—I was terrified of being paralyzed. At least in a wheelchair, I could flail my arms and shrug my shoulders. But in bed, I couldn't move at all except to turn my head on my pillow. My bed was an altar of affliction.

But time, prayer, and study in God's Word have a way of changing many things. And somewhere in the ensuing years, I discovered that the weakness of those claustrophobic hours was the key to God's peace and power. My enforced stillness was God's way of conforming the inside to what had happened on the outside.

Now, many years later, my bed is an altar of praise. It's the one spot on this harried planet where I always meet God in relaxed stillness. In fact, as soon as I wheel into my bedroom and see the bed covers pulled back my mind immediately responds, *It's time to be still and know more about God. It's time to pray.*

It can be the same for you. When you find yourself in forced stillness—waiting in line, sitting by a hospital bed, or stuck in traffic—instead of fidgeting and fuming, use such moments to practice stillness before God.

It's a crazy world and life speeds by at a blur, yet God is right in the middle of the craziness. And anywhere, at anytime, we may turn to Him, hear His voice, feel His hand, and catch the fragrance of heaven.

You can be still and know that He is God. And you don't have to break your neck to find out.

# HOLINESS...

## IN PEOPLE

## FIRST THINGS FIRST

hat's the most important thing you do, Joni?"

It was a press conference in Poland. My mind, like a computer, zipped through a list of possible answers: speaking . . . painting . . . writing . . . singing. I clicked off another list: campaigning against a euthanasia initiative on the state ballot, visiting cerebral palsied teenagers, delivering wheelchairs and Bibles to disabled people in Africa.

All of this is significant to me. Especially since it means

exhausting travel and long hours away from home. But what is most important to me? I smiled. Among all the options, I knew.

"Being a good wife to my husband." The group of twenty reporters chuckled. I guessed their thoughts. *She can't be serious. Her books are in so many languages . . . she's speaking here in Poland and in other countries around world. Surely she's being gratuitous.*

But all they had to do was watch me smile at Ken, seated at the back of the room. They had forgotten he was there, but not me. I'm *always* conscious of where he is. My disability requires it. If my bad hip needs an adjustment from long hours in my chair, I look for Ken— no one's hands help quite like his. If I start coughing, I look for him again—when he pounds on my back, others may think it's "wife abuse," but his heavy hand is exactly what I need.

> *Wives, submit to your husbands as to the Lord. For the husband is the head of the wife as Christ is the head of the church . . . . Husbands, love your wives, just as Christ loved the church.*
>
> **EPHESIANS**
> **5:22-25**

That's not all. I get to meet his needs, too. If someone bruises his ego with a "Hi there, Mr. Eareckson," Ken looks to me. If he's in a quandary about counseling one of his students, he'll seek my advice. And if he just wants to kick back and goof off, I'm a ready audience for his antics.

When I stand before Jesus, I will be judged first for my faithfulness in marriage. My commitment to my marriage vows places me in an utterly unique and profoundly significant relationship with the most important human being on earth—my spouse. And if I can't be faithful in loving my husband, how can I be faithful in a ministry to millions?

Being faithful to Ken means saying "no" to speaking at a Luis Palau crusade because the date conflicts with Ken's speech at his school's baccalaureate. It means scheduling overseas travel so I can always be in town to help him chaperon the prom. Buying *Hebrew National* hot dogs for dinner rather than the *Oscar Meyer* ones that I prefer. Waving him off to go fishing on Saturdays. It means calling him every night when I'm away and occasionally bringing home a small *omiagi*. (That's Japanese for a "little unexpected gift.")

Most of all, it means praying for Ken daily and in a specific way. Nothing bonds me closer to my husband than interceding for him. If I sense my passion waning or my emotions sagging, if I find myself pulling back from the demands of marriage, I pray—for Ken. Nothing ignites love for my husband faster.

Your circumstances may be different, but you can do the same. Just remember who is the most important person on earth. Your spouse . . . that one in a million.

# THE WARMTH OF HIS CALLING

Ithough I was a typical February visit to Chicago—cold. At least it was for me. The natives said it was balmy, but I was chilled-to-the-bone and no amount of coats or blankets could warm me up. I shivered my way through the weekend, longing for my back porch and the California sun.

The cold was made worse by the heaviness of my spirit. Somehow a sense of doubt had gripped me, like some strange virus. Though I had weathered the privileged demands of ministry for many years, a frontal assault on the assurance of my calling was underway. It was a siege of doubt. And I was cold.

But God had reserved a healing balm for my spirit. He applied it on Saturday night after my message at Moody's Founders Week. I proceeded to the bookstore, to my reserved spot before of a line of people waiting for an autograph. I felt timid and uneasy, not because I don't love people or love seeing their joy, but because it was late and I knew there would be kinks in my neck from holding my pen at an odd angle. It wasn't my typical approach to such sessions, but neither had it been a typical trip. "Please, Lord," I prayed, "hold me up."

His answer stood in front of me. It was the line. You see, it wasn't your typical autograph line of quiet, reserved customers. This line was made up of a fellowship of "less-than-able" saints. There were people in wheelchairs. Men using walkers. Women using canes. Homeless folks from the streets of Chicago, and moms with disabled kids.

It wasn't long before the line broke into a disorderly, motley crew of joy seekers. The place was noisy with spirited conversations. Someone was always laughing. No one minded if the line wasn't quite as organized as the manager might have liked. A mentally disabled boy even cut in line to give me a hug.

I imagined this was much like those days with Jesus. He had always enjoyed the unruly but precious crowds in Palestine. And I knew He was equally delighted with this rag-tag line in a downtown bookstore.

Then it dawned on me. The line was God's gift to me . . . unwrapped and presented in all its noisy, chaotic glory. For a

*Let all we do be well done, fit for Thine eye to see.*

**GEORGE DAWSON**

34

while I had forgotten that the Lord who said, "Go," was the same Lord who said, "I am with you always." The very people He had called me to serve stood in that line. I had doubted the mission and the means of God, but now I embraced the warmth of His promise and His presence.

I was learning something important: we are most vulnerable to the piercing winds of doubt when we distance ourselves from the mission and fellowship to which Christ has called us. Our night of discouragement will seem endless, our task impossible, unless we recognize that He stands in our midst.

So get in line, my friend. Come join us.

Christ is with us . . . and the warmth is contagious.

# THE LITTLE GIRL AND THE GIFT

**H**oliness is often hidden—no, I take that back—is often showcased in a child. Take the time I was in an airport drugstore in Hawaii. Ken was at the ticket counter, and I was using the time to pick up a few last-minute gifts for friends. I found a clerk in one of the aisles who helped stack three boxes of chocolate-covered macadamia nuts on my lap.

When I wheeled up to the cashier's counter, I learned that the total for my purchase was $17.89. I asked the clerk to reach into my handbag, get my wallet, and take out a ten-dollar bill and seven ones. "If you don't mind counting it out, I have enough change to make the 89 cents."

"Sure," the clerk replied. When she opened up the coin purse of my wallet and saw all my pennies, she asked if I'd like to get rid of them. I glanced around to make certain I wouldn't be holding up any other customers. "Great!" I replied.

And so, while standing next to me and holding my wallet open so I could see, she proceeded to dig for pennies and count them out on the counter one-by-one.

Suddenly, a little girl darted up and—clink!—very delicately dropped a penny into my change purse. "O-oh," I gasped. But before I had a chance to react, she dashed back to the card rack to her daddy's side. The clerk and I looked at each other with surprise and pleasure. "What was *that* all about?" she asked.

While the clerk bagged my chocolates, I put two and two together. The little girl must have been watching me the

whole time from behind her daddy's legs. When she saw the clerk rummaging through my wallet to help me find change to pay my bill, she must have thought I was poor and didn't have enough money to pay my bill. *Should I go over to the card rack and tell her the truth?* I asked myself. *Should I tell her I didn't need her penny? How should I respond?*

With the bag on my lap, I wheeled over to the child, smiled and said, "I want to thank you very much for helping me." I caught her dad's eye and added, "You have the wonderful quality of compassion, and if you don't know what that means, ask your daddy and he will tell you." Her father gave me a wink.

> *A gift opens the way for the giver and ushers him into the presence of the great.*
> **PROVERBS 18:16**

As I left the store, I realized it was not only the right response, it was the only response. Although I didn't need her gift, reinforcing her generosity was more important than rectifying her impressions. If a child wants to be generous and compassionate at my expense, fine. If it helps her to think I'm in desperate need of her gift, fine.

God was surely looking down and smiling that day. A child's generous spirit was reinforced, and her compassion encouraged. A father was made proud. And God received the glory.

A little thoughtfulness—even a penny's worth—goes a long way.

# WHENEVER YOU EAT THE BREAD

esterday was a day to remember. It was the day to celebrate communion —at least in my church. So literally, it was a day of remembrance. It's curious that God didn't command any sacrament to commemorate His birth, life, miracles, or resurrection. Only His death.

For me, the Lord's Supper is always a powerful visual symbol. Maybe it's because we actually handle the bread and lift the wine to our lips. Yet as the plate of crackers is passed, we're ever so careful to lift our little "pinkie" and aim for our cracker without touching any of the others. Our fastidious care, although tidy, also seems symbolic: we go to such extraordinary efforts to live our lives totally isolated from each other, even though we are *one* in Christ.

I thought about this when I watched Teddy, an autistic teenager, reach toward the communion plate. I saw him eye the plate. He groaned with delight (he can't speak) and leaned his large frame forward. His muscles twitched, his hand grabbed, and before his mother could stop him, he held up a fat fistful of pieces of cracker. "Teddy, no!" his mother hoarsely whispered. "You're only supposed to take *one!*"

Teddy guffawed and proudly held up a squeezed mash of crackers. His mother was embarrassed, but I could hardly stifle the giggles. Unlike the rest of us, he felt no shame in touching other peoples' crackers.

I thought of that when my friend sitting next to me reached into the plate to get crackers for both of us. Then, after the pastor invited us all to participate, she lifted one piece to my mouth and then, the other piece to hers. I can't take communion by myself. I'm a little . . . no . . . a lot like Teddy. I'm forced to depend on another Christian to handle my bread for me.

I'm glad about that. It makes me feel connected. Interdependent. One with others. It's a happy symbol of how closely I must live my life with fellow believers. I can't live my life alone and isolated.

Communion celebrates the body of Christ, broken on the cross. Communion celebrates the Body of Christ, the Church. Communion is a celebration of unity.

Oh, how I wish we'd remember important things like this when the bread and wine are passed.

> *Whenever you eat this bread and drink this cup, you proclaim the Lord's death until he comes.*
>
> **1 CORINTHIANS 11:26**

# MAKE ME A BLESSING

Out in the highways and byways of life,
Many are weary and sad;
Carry the sunshine where darkness is rife,
Making the sorrowing glad.

Chorus:
Make me a blessing,
Make me a blessing,
Out of my life may Jesus shine;
Make me a blessing, O Savior I pray,
Make me a blessing to someone today.

Tell the sweet story of Christ and His love,
Tell of His pow'r to forgive
Others will trust Him if only you prove
True, every moment you live.

Give as 'twas given to you in your need,
Love as the Master loved you;
Be to the helpless a helper indeed,
Unto your mission be true.

Text: Ira B. Wilson
Music: George S. Schuler

# KEEPING SABBATH WITH A FRIEND

**W**hen it comes to Sundays, I was raised right. Gather the laundry off the clothesline. Turn off the television. Put away homework. Clear away the pots and pans. And the important one my parents always enforced—no shopping!

Forty years have passed, and I have my own house to keep now. Modern times have ushered in certain conveniences that help me abide by these Sunday observances. Most people don't have clotheslines strung across their backyards, and one can easily stow plates and bowls in the dishwasher. But there is one modern convenience that doesn't help. It hinders. I'm tempted by the Topanga Plaza Mall. When I was a kid, there were no malls. Five-and-Dimes, as well as Sears, shut their doors on Sundays. Today it's a different story.

For the most part, I steer clear of Sunday purchases. If I do go to the mall, I usually bypass the sales racks. But I will open my wallet for a glazed treat from Cinnabon and a cup of Starbucks. Still, it feels odd to be in the "market place" on Sundays.

Last week when my friend Mary Jean came to town for a visit, I shelved my guilt and took her for a meander through the mall after church. Mary Jean travels long hours and works hard in ministry like I do, so what better way for us to relax than to do something "normal"? We got as far as the coffee bar outside of Nordstroms. We sat, sipping our cafe lattes, cooing at babies in strollers, and admiring all the nicely dressed women sauntering by.

We talked. Mostly about outreach efforts for families affected by disability. I told Mary Jean about Bonnie, a young lady living at Magnolia Gardens Nursing Home. "Bonnie's neuro-muscular disease has advanced to the point where she lies in bed all day," I told Mary Jean. "It'd be good if we could spend some time praying for her today. I've heard she's been very depressed lately."

My voice trailed off. Mary Jean tapped her coffee straw. For a long moment, we said nothing. Then our eyes met . . . and we said simultaneously, "What are we doing *here?*"

We gathered our things and scurried toward a phone. Yes, Bonnie was able to receive visitors. No, we wouldn't be intruding. Bonnie didn't have many friends dropping by.

We made a beeline for the parking lot. The half-hour drive was filled with praying, singing hymns, and reading Scripture. We pulled into the shaded driveway of the little nursing home and hurried down the dimly lit hallways. Bonnie's room was the last one on the right.

Her eyes lit up when she saw us. She couldn't communicate much through her stiffened smile. Breath and words didn't come easily. But that didn't daunt Mary Jean and I. We sang to Bonnie and occasionally sat quietly, enjoying the birds chirping outside the window. Finally, at the close of our visit, I asked if Bonnie would like to repeat the Lord's Prayer with us. Expressionless, she nodded. While a bedpan clattered to the floor down the hallway and people chattered at the nurses' station, we united our hearts and spoke to our Father.

> *To [those] who keep my Sabbaths, who choose what pleases me and hold fast to my covenant—these I will bring to my holy mountain and give them joy in my house of prayer.*
>
> **ISAIAH 56:4, 7**

Mary Jean did many things during her visit. She enjoyed a jaunt to the beach and an evening out at a fancy restaurant. But the highlight was that marvelous chance to keep the Sabbath with a friend in need.

There will always be a sale at Nordstroms . . . but there won't always be an opportunity to *"redeem the time."* Especially on a Sunday. Especially since Bonnie passed on to glory just a few months later.

hy am I living?"
"What's my purpose?"
Not many people
have the guts to say it out loud, but lots of us think it.
There's a slew of self-help books, mid-day talk shows, and
one-hour counseling services to help us find meaning and
purpose. Sometimes the purpose is hard to pin down in this
quick-fix, fast-paced, no-deposit-no-return culture. Everything's
so external. Disposable. Even people who seem to have no
purpose in living.

Case in point—Cody. He was born with the umbilical
cord wrapped around his neck, leaving him totally paralyzed
and unable to speak. He is completely deaf and blind. He
needs a ventilator in order to breathe and a feeding tube in
order to eat. All this baggage attached to a little seventeen-
month-old boy.

I met Cody at one of our recent JAF Ministries Family
Retreats. His foster parents provide care for him and two
other handicapped children. After one of our evening
sessions, I wheeled up to Cody's mother at the snack shack.
She was enjoying an ice cream cone and gently moving
Cody's stroller back and forth. They seemed the perfect
picture of contentment.

I parked next to them and joined the quiet moment of
contentment. Looking at her foster son, I asked the obvious
question: "How are you able to connect with him?"

She tossed away the end of the cone and wiped her
fingers. "When Cody cries, I'll gently brush his cheek," she
explained, showing me as she lovingly touched his face with

the backside of her hand, " . . . and he'll stop right away. This lets me know he's alert."

I leaned over to do the same. I couldn't feel his cheek, but it looked good. Plus, as I stroked him, I thought I saw a faint smile. I prayed silently, asking God to be large in Cody's heart, to comfort and console him, to speak, "not in words taught us by human wisdom but in words taught by the Spirit" (1 Cor. 2:13).

I thought of those who would say, "Take out his feeding tube. Let him starve to death. His life has no meaning, no purpose." But 2 Corinthians 5:16 warns us to "regard no one from a worldly point of view." Elsewhere we are reminded that "inwardly we are being renewed day by day. For our light and momentary troubles are achieving for us an eternal glory that far outweighs them all. So we fix our eyes not on what is seen, but on what is unseen" (2 Cor. 4:16-18).

> *God is a tranquil being and abides in a tranquil eternity. So must your spirit become a tranquil and clear little pool, wherein the serene light of God can be mirrored.*
>
> **GERHARD TERSTEEGEN**

God's Word is as true for Cody as it is for anyone. The Spirit expresses truth to him—not in audible words, but in spiritual words. Inwardly he is being renewed. His troubles are achieving for him an eternal glory. His value is "not on what is seen, but on what is unseen." Therefore, we are not to regard him from a worldly point of view.

The Spirit is dynamic, active, and powerful, and although we can't see the spiritual activity happening in Cody's life, it's there. His is a hidden holiness. We can't measure God's work, or quantify it—but it's real. And spiritual activity gives life value, no matter how humble a person's situation.

Cody isn't doing much more than living and being. But God has His reasons. He has His purposes. Ours is an intentional God, brimming over with motive and mission. He never does things capriciously or decides with the flip of a coin. And His design for that little boy is to simply live, breathe, and encourage others.

It's enough to give life meaning and purpose.

# THE FRESH AIR OF POSSIBILITIES

I'm a quadriplegic, yet I can drive a van. (It doesn't have a steering wheel. My hand is secured to a big joy stick so I can steer, accelerate, and brake . . . but wait, that's another story.) That I drive should tell you I enjoy being independent. If there's something I can do, I will. Even if it means doing the Drive-Thru at Burger King by myself.

Remember, my hands don't work. That's why last week when I cruised into the drive-thru lane to order hamburgers and cokes, I prayed. Not so much for me, but for the fellows at the pick-up window. *Lord, give them patience . . . and give me a smile.* Then I moved up to the intercom to give my order.

When I had finished explaining "no cheese" and "extra mustard packets," I told the voice on the other end of the intercom that I was disabled. "But don't worry," I leaned toward the big black box, "I'll explain to the guys at the delivery window what to do." There was a pause. Then "Okay . . . no problem."

I pulled up to the delivery window and smiled. Sticking my arm out the window, I asked the cashier fellow to take the ten-dollar bill that was folded in my arm splint. That was a cinch. While he fished for my change, I asked him to place it in the paper bag along with the hamburgers. At that point, the server who was bagging my order looked over his shoulder. Both boys, confused, gave each other a look that said, *Do you know what she's talking about? 'Cause I don't!* I smiled and slowly repeated my instructions.

Both servers got the message. They even wrapped the change in a napkin before they dropped it into the bag with the food. Then they handed me my order, but I had to ask, "Could you please lean out of your window and wedge the bag right here between me and the van door?" Both boys looked at each other again. "I can't reach for the bag. Remember? I can't use my hands."

"Oh yeah," they laughed and proceeded to hang halfway out the pick-up window in order to lodge the package between my wheelchair and the door. "Are you set? Are you okay?" they asked in genuine sincerity. "Great job," I assured them. "God bless you guys!" They slapped the side of my van as I drove off. I glanced in my rearview mirror—they were waving goodbye. *Thanks, Lord, for answering prayer. That could have been an awkward situation for those two boys, but it turned out to be fun!*

> *How little people know who think that holiness is dull. When one meets the real thing . . . it is irresistible.*
>
> **C. S. LEWIS**

This is the daily stuff of my life. It always involves more than simply picking up hamburgers and cokes, or clothes from the dry cleaners. It involves a chance to make God real to people. A chance for them to serve, to feel good about themselves, to experience a "new way of doing things." It's a chance to break the mold and accomplish a task in a different manner—an opportunity to throw a hand-grenade into the ordinary way of living and, in so doing, take people by surprise. (Those fellows at Burger King learned a lot about flexibility and adaptability, as well as customer satisfaction.)

We all have expectations. We want people to conform and comply, fall in line and follow suit. "Don't rock the boat." That's our motto. "Don't do things differently. Don't create a

scene and don't cause a ruckus." Yet problems are often God's way of grabbing a lever in order to pry us out of our ruts. And when you rise up out of a rut, you end up enjoying the fresh air of possibilities, the new breeze of challenge and change. Your faith finds feet. Your witness begins to work. You are "brought into the glorious freedom of the children of God" (Rom. 8:21).

Today, take a complicated situation and with time, patience, and a smile, turn it into something positive . . . for you and for others.

## MARY ROSE

It happened minutes before I was called up to the platform to address the overflowing convention. My friend straightened my collar, artfully messed with my hair, and stood back to give me one last check. I took a deep breath, emptying my mind of the morning's interviews and telephone calls. I had worked hard on the message I was about to give to the thousands gathered. A stagehand fussed with my lapel microphone. My friend paced. The air behind the platform was heavy with importance.

That's when I met Mary Rose. She shuffled toward me, leaning on the arm of her escort. Her gait was stiff, and her arm was curled against her chest. I guessed she had cerebral palsy. She wore a tan cardigan over a yellow cotton dress. Nothing fancy. Her glasses sat askew on her nose. "Joni," her escort said, "this is my friend Mary Rose, and she's been waiting for so long to meet you."

She startled me. Didn't these two women understand I was trying to concentrate? Mary Rose didn't sense a thing, but stretched out her rigid arm to greet me. Her body may have been stiff, but her smile was anything but. It was warm and relaxed. She was excited to meet me, the author of a book that had meant so much to her decades earlier. "And Joni," her escort said, "Mary Rose has something to tell you that will encourage you as you speak today."

*If but ten among us lead a holy life, we shall kindle a fire which shall light up the entire city.*

**ST. JOHN CHRYSOSTOM**

*It better be important,* I thought.

"I've been praying . . . for you . . . every day," she said slowly and with great effort, "ever since . . . I read your book." She wavered and steadied herself on the arm of my chair. Rather stunned, I let that fact sink in. *Praying for me? Every day?* Mary Rose guessed my thoughts. She repeated, "I've been praying . . . every day." My irritation evaporated. I did some messy math in my head and came up with more than 7,000 days of prayer. Seven thousand times this woman had lifted me up to the Savior—and she had never met me!

"May . . . I pray . . . for you now?" she asked and then bowed her head. Afterward, as I watched her slowly shuffle away, I thought of Jesus' words, "Well done, good and faithful

*Holiness in People*

servant! You have been faithful with a few things. . . . Come and share your Master's happiness!" (Matt. 25:23).

Mary Rose slipped silently into the shadows, while I wheeled out into the light. But I didn't feel all that important. Good thing. God is by no means impressed that I can paint with my mouth, have written books, traveled all over the

world, or am on speaking terms with Billy Graham. He doesn't get effusive and say, "I'm sure proud of her. Chalk another one up for the lady in the wheelchair." I'm not discounting my painting, books, or the exciting places I've served. I just feel that I've already received a lot of my reward—the reward of seeing the gospel go forth because of this chair.

When it comes to "entering the Master's happiness," the highest accolades will go—and should go—to godly people who have labored loyally yet received no recognition. The grand and glorious purposes for my suffering are clear to all, but some dear saints have struggled without a boost from anyone. Mary Rose's ministry is not "up front" but in her secret closet of prayer. She intercedes without applause or attention. Not only does no one notice, few care.

I may have stood up to the vicissitudes of human hardship, such as pain and paralysis, but Mary Rose's strength of spirit and faithfulness in service more than match—even surpass—mine. When she receives her reward, I'll stand happily on the sidelines, cheering and whistling.

That's what I love about serving God. In His eyes, there are no little people . . . because there are no big people. We are all on the same playing field. We all start at square one. No one has it better than the other, or possesses unfair advantage.

Success in a ministry or a marriage is not the key. Faithfulness is.

# HOLINESS...

# IN HIDDEN·

# PLACES

# A LOVE AFFAIR IN THE NIGHT

 have an ongoing love affair with the night sky. When there's a full moon, I make a beeline for the backyard to look for moon shadows. And if the winds are cool and brisk—as they are this time of year—I'm outside with my star chart, saying goodbye to summertime constellations. Although the September night sky is beautiful and still vibrates with the splashy echo of summer's constellations, the seasons are changing. And so is the sky.

But one thing won't change. I will forever hold close to my heart an encounter I had with the night sky and the Comet of 1996. That's when the Hyakutake Comet whizzed by Earth and lit up the bottom half of the Big Dipper for six glorious nights. Ken and I squinted into the heavens from our backyard, but the lights of the San Fernando Valley obscured our view. I read the next day in the *Los Angeles Times* that the best place for comet viewing was far beyond Los Angeles.

So the next evening, when the comet was to be its brightest, we piled into the van and raced north. Highway 14 climbs out of the Los Angeles basin, up over the San Gabriel Mountains, and flattens out on a high desert plateau. When we got to that broad expanse, we turned off the highway onto a dirt road winding up into the Tehachapi Mountains, which edge the Mojave Desert. We parked near the summit, got out, and looked up. I sat breathless.

The moon made a thin smile on the horizon, and the stars were dusted like powdered sugar on black velvet. In the cold desert air, everything was crisp and clear. No haze, no city lights, no smog, and *definitely* no noise. Just the wispy sound of air moving through the pine trees—no, I take that back, we did catch the hooting of a couple of owls.

The heavy silence of the desert made the sparkling night sky all the more dramatic. How could something so big be so quiet? And there, after our eyes adjusted to the dark, just below the Big Dipper, was the comet. A fuzzy ball of light 9.5 million miles away.

And could it be? Yes, it was! After almost thirty minutes we saw the long, thin tail of the comet—cutting like a laser through the Big Dipper and touching the edge of a distant constellation.

We had stepped onto the backside of Elijah's chariot, whooshed away by the glorious sight. It seemed like the Lord of the universe was beckoning us, whispering, "Want to see my glory? Come up to the top of this mountain. Let me peel back the stratosphere so you can take a peek at the marvels of my creation. A sign in the sky. An omen of my power."

We couldn't stifle our excitement. And so, on the side of the mountain, under a blanket of stars, we shook the night air with rousing song, harmonizing on a wonderful verse from "Praise My Soul, the King of Heaven,"

> *Angels help us to adore Him,*
> *Ye behold Him face to face.*
> *Sun and moon bow down before Him . . .*

An hour and ten hymns later, we reluctantly packed up and headed back. When we returned home, we lifted mugs of hot chocolate over a star chart of constellations in a "toast" to the next 10,000 years. That's right. The Hyakatuke Comet won't pass by again for another ten millenia. It was a once-in-a-lifetime event. Little wonder as Ken and I got ready for bed, we found ourselves humming, "Sun, moon, and stars in their courses above, join with all nature in manifold witness, to God's great faithfulness, mercy and love."

Try it tonight. Go outside and look for your moon shadow. Take a star chart and spot a few constellations. Read Psalm 8:3 and pray,

> *When I consider your heavens . . .*
> *what is man that you are mindful of him?*

It's a great way to start a love affair with the sky.

# SOMEBODY NEEDS HELP

he gate of iron crossbars clanged behind me. Immediately a flood of memories washed over me. I smiled weakly at the guard who sat encased in a metal perch behind a thick protective window. He looked a little like the uniformed guard who used to sit at the front door of the rehab center where I lived for two years.

As I wheeled into the next prison block, I couldn't get over the irony. Here I was confined by my own set of bolts and bars, yet free-wheeling. And these men, though free to walk and use their hands, were confined behind bars.

I had come to cut the ribbon on JAF Ministries' Wheels for the World restoration center where prisoners refurbish used wheelchairs for our teams to deliver overseas to disabled children and adults. The inmates had seen our video of disabled children who lived on straw mats or in wheelbarrows. Each child was given a new set of wheels—wheelchairs refurbished by these prisoners.

I entered the restoration center and gasped. There was row after row of sturdy wooden shelves filled with neatly stacked wheelchairs, footrests, armrests, and walkers. Everything was tidy and organized.

I flashed a smile at four inmates who stood proudly by their workbenches, polishing chrome and screwing on new leather backing to chair-frames. It was Ephesians 4:28 in action: "He who has been stealing must steal no longer, but must work, doing something useful with his own hands, that he may have something to share with those in need."

"Uh . . . mind if I ask you to do a bit of detail work on these leg-rests of mine?" I asked as I gestured toward the chipped paint on the legs of my chair. I wheeled closer so one of them could take a look. "You men are doing such a fantastic job," I said, eyeing the completed chairs, shined and ready for shipment. "I'd trust you with this chair any day!" I could have had the wheelchair repair service back home spruce up my wheels, but I needed a bridge to these inmates.

> *Do not withhold good from those who deserve it, when it is in your power to act.*
>
> **PROVERBS 3:27**

"I'll have it done in thirty minutes," said Jorge. With that, he began sanding my leg-rests and preparing the paint.

I watched for a moment, then asked, "Why are you doing this?" He gave me a funny look. "No, I mean *this*," I gestured toward

the wooden shelves, racks of tools, and wheelchairs waiting to be worked on.

Jorge fiddled with his wrench for a moment. "Because somebody needs help," he said simply, as if the answer were obvious. "It makes me feel good to do something that's gonna help somebody. Like those kids in that video." He shrugged his shoulders good-naturedly and went back to work.

I left the prison that day with a fresh resolve to "do something that's gonna help somebody." Because in a lonely prison there are men who see the value of helping others to be free from their "prisons." Men who are willing to turn down a minimum-wage job in the prison work program to volunteer their time restoring chairs . . . in order to restore someone's life. Men who are being successfully rehabilitated, *"doing something useful"* so that they *"have something to share with those in need."*

I can do something useful. I have something to share with someone in need . . . and you do, too!

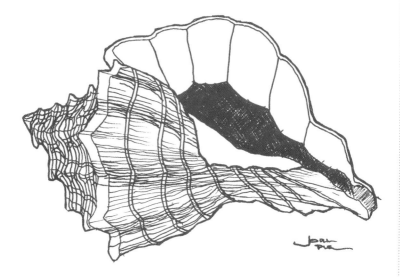

## A QUIET CALM
## BENEATH THE WAVES

A warm breeze touched my cheek the other day and took me back to sunny childhood memories of camping in the sand dunes near Ocean City, Maryland. Our days were spent splashing in the surf, collecting shells, or digging for clams along the inlet. At sundown, we would shake the sand off our thongs, pile into Dad's old truck, and head to the Dairy Queen at Dewey Beach, where we'd sit on the tailgate, lick ice cream cones, and watch the sun set over the inlet. If it wasn't too late, we'd drive across the state line to Delaware and enjoy a nighttime stroll along the boardwalk at Rehoboth. My sisters

and I would sit on a bench and eat saltwater taffy while watching people go by.

Long after dark we kids would fall asleep on the way back to camp. Later, after snuggling into my sleeping bag under the mosquito netting, I'd drift off again listening to the roar of the breakers . . . the crashing, pounding, and shush-shingling of receding water over tiny pebbles.

*Be still and know that I am God.*

**PSALM 46:10**

The next morning, after the sun was high and hot, my sisters and I would don our bathing suits and head for the water. It was nothing for us to spend an entire afternoon in the ocean, playing catch with the waves. The deafening sound of powerful breakers thrilled, yet frightened me. Yet when I swam beyond the breakers, I was amazed at how subdued the crashing waves sounded. When I dove beneath the surface, the underwater acoustics made the thunderous roar seem distant and gentle.

It's been many years since those day of camping in the dunes, but I can still hear the sound of those waves. My heart swelled with that sound recently when I read a poem by Frances Havergal. She must have sat on the beaches of Maryland when she wrote,

> On the surface foam and roar,
> Restless heave and passionate dash,
> Shingle rattle on the shore,
> Gathering boom and thundering crash.
> Under the surface, soft green light,
> A hush of peace and an endless calm,
> Winds and waves from a choral height,
> Falling sweet as a far off psalm.

*Holiness . . . in Hidden Places*

She's right. Though there's a majestic and powerful beauty on the surface of the ocean, there's even more beauty when you dive beneath the waves. Even as a kid with a face mask on, I'd dive and discover a world of endless calm—luxuriant seaweed swaying gracefully, colorful shells, small fish darting here and there . . . a world that's quiet and deep.

When you dive beneath the surface things of God, you also discover an endless calm—a world of divine life that is quiet and deep. There, in the depths, God will reveal a quiet and gentle kind of interior beauty.

The Lord is so generous! Even when we choose to live only on the surface of things, where we're often tossed this way and that, God still reveals Himself through thrilling displays of His power. But there's much more to God than what you see—what we all see of Him—on the surface.

When we dive deeper into God's heart, all the turmoil of our daily lives—the problems that crash around us like huge waves—seem somehow . . . distant. The roar is like a far-away echo of thunderous waves "falling sweet as a far off psalm." And in closing, I think I'll let my seashore friend, Frances Havergal, take you for a deeper dive . . .

> *There are strange, soul depths,*
> *Restless and vast, unfathomed as the sea.*
> *An infinite craving for some infinite stilling.*
> *And, lo, His perfect love is perfect filling.*
> *Lord Jesus Christ, my Lord and my God,*
> *Thou, thou art enough for me.*

# WHERE JESUS IS

To walk where Jesus walked is a thrill. I know. I've been there . . . to Israel, that is. I've wheeled the cobbled streets of old Jerusalem and touched the Western Wall. I've wandered through the village of Bethany and sat outside the home of Mary, Martha, and Lazarus. I've peered into a gorge and followed the caravan trail that twists from Jerusalem to Jericho. Oh, to walk the paths Christ walked . . . to see the sights He saw.

I thought about this when my husband, Ken, stood on the spot where Jesus preached the Sermon on the Mount. We parked our van overlooking the Sea of Galilee and wandered through a field to a natural amphitheater tucked on the side of the hill. It was late in the day. All the tour buses were gone, and the hillside was quiet. A breeze rustled a tree nearby. Ken drew a deep breath, stretched his arms wide and said, "Oh, to be where Jesus was!" Looking up at him, I smiled in reply.

Ken stood facing the west, gazing across the north edge of the lake toward Tiberias and Mt. Tabor. The sky was large and wide, ablaze from the setting sun. With a dry wind whipping his hair, he clasped his hands behind his back, faced the glowing sky and began to recite Jesus' words: "Blessed are the poor in spirit, for theirs is the kingdom of heaven. Blessed are those who mourn, for they will be comforted . . ."

The wind carried Ken's words, caressing the land with the same beatitudes Christ once pronounced over the hill. "Blessed are those who hunger and thirst for righteousness, for they will be filled . . . Blessed are the peacemakers, for they will be called sons of God . . ."

> *I have been crucified with Christ and I no longer live, but Christ lives in me.*
>
> **GALATIANS 2:20**

As Ken slowly recited the sermon, picking up speed as he went, I was gripped. Not so much by the thought of being where Jesus was but where He *is*, right now, shining through the eyes of my husband, resonating through every fiber of Ken's being, filling his life with virtue and courage. True, Jesus once lived among these hills, but He's living now as Ken gives voice to His words. Even after Ken concluded his recitation my eyes kept misting . . . oh, to be where Jesus *is*!

Yes, to be where Jesus was, is heartwarming. That He's coming back is heart-pumping. But the most powerful reality is that *Jesus is.* He is the great I AM living in the present tense, sustaining everything by the power of His word. It says so in Revelation 11:17, "We give you thanks, O Lord God Almighty, the One who is and who was and who is to come . . ." (NKJV). Notice the order. The past and the future don't rank first, but the present. It's not "was, is, and is to come," but "is, was, and is to come."

God *is.* The present reality of Christ pulsing and breathing life and vitality into our souls is matchless. The past and the present can't touch it. I know. I saw it that day on a hill above the Sea of Galilee.

# O MASTER, LET ME WALK WITH THEE

O Master, let me walk with Thee
In lowly paths of service free;
Tell me Thy secret;
Help me bear the strain of toil, the fret of care.

Help me the slow of heart to move
By some clear, winning word of love;
Teach me the wayward feet to stay,
And guide them in the homeward way.

Teach me Thy patience;
Still with Thee in closer, dearer company,
In work that keeps faith sweet and strong,
In trust that triumphs over wrong.

In hope that sends a shining ray
Far down the future's broadening way,
In peace that only Thou can'st give,
With Thee, O Master, let me live.

Lyrics: Washington Gladden, 1879
Music: H. Percy Smith, 1874

he year is 1967. I am 17 years old. Stuck. Paralyzed on a Stryker frame in the geriatric ward of a state institution. The dark-shadowed room can't match the black cloud hanging over me. I am desperate, looking for a miracle. What young girl lying numb and motionless with tubes running in and out of her wouldn't? *Oh God, will you please heal me?* I whisper, crying in the night.

It was the first time I had prayed for an out-and-out miracle—a prayer prompted by a friend who had sat by my bedside earlier in the day reading the passage from John 5 about the man at the Pool of Bethesda.

> Now there is in Jerusalem near the Sheep Gate a pool, which in Aramaic is called Bethesda. . . . One who was there had been an invalid for thirty-eight years. When Jesus saw him lying there and learned that he had been in this condition for a long time, he asked him, "Do you want to get well?" "Sir," the invalid replied, "I have no one to help me into the pool when the water is stirred. . . ." Then Jesus said to him, "Get up! Pick up your mat and walk." At once the man was cured; he picked up his mat and walked.

It was the part about being an invalid for thirty-eight years that got me. *Please, Lord, I can't live without the use of my hands or legs for three days, let alone thirty years! I'm not like that man by the Pool at Bethesda. Be compassionate to me, like you were to him. Heal me!*

I imagined myself among the many that day when Jesus walked by the pool. I saw the columns and tiled porches. I felt the dry, dusty air. There I was, lying on a straw mat, Jesus' eyes meeting mine, His heart sensing my desperation. Stepping over others to kneel by my mat, He reaches down in compassion, touching my cheek and—yes!—saying, "Daughter, be healed." The power of the image caused a muscle spasm, and my body shook in anticipation. *Oh, God, yes, I believe you want to heal me. I believe! Raise me up, I ask you, put me in the pool, too!*

I strained to rise from my Stryker. But my legs and hands never got the message.

The year is 1998. More than thirty years have passed since that dark night in the hospital. I abandoned long ago those desperate times of prayer, those urgent pleadings that Jesus might heal me, too, like the man at the Pool of Bethesda.

And suddenly, I'm here. Not healed, but here at the actual Pool. Ken and I are vacationing in Israel, touring Jerusalem, and without knowing it, we turn a cobblestone corner and—oh, my goodness—here's the pool . . . the ruins of the five colonnades . . . the steps leading down to the water. I look around and in my mind's eye see hundreds of sick and paralyzed people. I turn to Ken and remark, "You wouldn't believe how many times I used to picture myself here." I scan the ruins and murmur, "And now . . . after thirty years . . . I'm *here*."

Tears well up in my eyes. "I made it," I say weakly, resting my arm on the guardrail. "Jesus *didn't* pass me by. He *didn't* overlook me. He answered my prayer—He said 'No.'"

And I'm glad. A "no" answer has purged sin from my life, strengthened my commitment to Christ, and forced me to depend on grace. It has bound me with other believers, produced discernment, disciplined my mind, and taught me to spend my time wisely. It has stretched my hope, increased my faith, and strengthened my character. Being in this wheelchair has meant knowing Christ better. Feeling His strength every day.

The noonday sun is high and a brisk wind dries my tears. Nobody is at the Pool this time of day. The quiet moment becomes a milestone, an altar of remembrance. The Lord brought me here that I might tell Him—no, that I might thank Him—for the wiser choice, the better answer, the richer path. "And, Lord," I say out loud, gazing at the dusty, bare porticos and imagining them crowded with the many that day who did not get healed, "thank you for giving me the chance to tell others that sometimes 'no' is a better answer. Sometimes healing happens on the inside."

"Are you okay?" Ken touches my cheek.

"Yes," I sniff and laugh. I can't believe I'm crying and laughing at the same time. There *are* more important things in life than walking.

## THE BUGGY RIDE

own against the
southern edge of
Pennsylvania sits the
hamlet of Bird-in-Hand. It's Amish country. The hills are
gentle, and fields stretch out like a patchwork quilt where
meandering streams divide one farm from the next. We
drove slowly down Church Lane past a couple of horse-
drawn buggies. When we got to the one-room schoolhouse,
we turned right into the driveway of John and Rebecca
Stoltzfus' home. Rebecca, wearing a black dress, apron, and a
white hat, waved from the back porch, spoon in hand. We
were right on time for a country dinner.

The Stoltzfus children, in the same Amish garb, smiled a
warm welcome. They had set up extra tables. It was a good
thing. The home was abuzz with extra help in the kitchen, as
well as a couple of farm neighbors who had dropped by to

*Holiness...in Hidden Places*

say "hello." After John blessed the food, bowls of creamed corn and applesauce, creamed celery and Pennsylvania Dutch noodles were passed this way and that. Homemade jam. Creamery butter. Ham cakes and fried chicken.

When we finished shoo-fly pie, we carried our glasses of lemonade to the backyard and sat under a spreading elm tree to enjoy the golden glow of late afternoon. Scents of new-mown hay and cow pastures wafted in the breeze. "Let's sing hymns!" I offered. "Do you know any German hymns?" The Stoltzfus family and their friends made a group, all with straw hats and white head-coverings. We sat opposite and made an English-singing choir. Back and forth we sang, one hymn after the next—we in English, they in German.

After songs, it was chatting and more pie. "How about a buggy ride?" John's son, Elmer, asked, peering at me from under his straw hat. Elmer was in a wheelchair like me, and I thought his question was odd. Didn't he know my wheelchair would never fit in a buggy? He gave a knowing look and motioned me toward the barn. There his brother was harnassing up Hank the horse and hitching him to the buggy.

Not just any buggy. John Stoltzfus unlatched the back, and it flipped down to make a ramp. "Wheel right on in," he laughed. I couldn't wipe the silly grin off my face—I hadn't ridden in a buggy for years, let alone an Amish one. I wheeled up the ramp and into the backside of the carriage, then wedged my chair tightly between the driver's seat and the side.

Elmer's wife, Sarah, climbed up into the seat. She grabbed Hank's reins and with a click-click, turned our horse and buggy toward Church Lane. She reined Hank right at the

> *Keep your lives free from the love of money and be content with what you have.*
>
> **HEBREWS 13:5**

schoolhouse, and we clip-clopped up the road at a slow trot. We passed school boys in black hats and suspendered-trousers. We waved at barefoot little girls holding hands by milk cans at the end of a farm lane.

The sun was quickly descending behind a hill, casting a misty rose-colored haze over the fields. Fireflies were beginning to light up along a stream. The air was sweet, the moment, fragrant. I kept thinking, though, of living without radios, electric lights, air-conditioning and heating. Having no modern kitchen

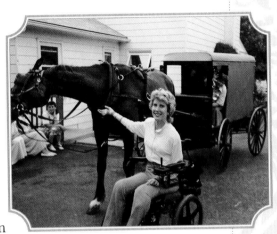

appliances or washing machines. I turned to Sarah, "Would you ever want to leave here? You and Elmer?"

The lovely young woman with the white cap and wide smile gave me the same knowing look her husband had earlier. She gestured toward rows of green corn beside dairy barns, buggy sheds, and flocks of white geese. "Why would we leave this?" She didn't need to say anymore. We smiled at one another and let the countryside do the talking.

Holiness isn't in a style of dress. It's not a matter of rules and regulations. It's a way of life that emanates quietness and rest, joy in family, shared pleasures with friends, the help of a neighbor—and the hope of a Savior.

Holiness is found in many hidden places. It can also be found along Church Lane outside of Bird-in-Hand in Lancaster County, Pennsylvania.

# A WALL OF HOSTILITY

nyone who reads the papers, knows the story of Bosnia. It's a splintered society with towns separated by barbed wire, concrete emplacements, and fields of land mines. We had come to this fractured country to offer hope and help to those disabled from the war. It was a challenge. More than 1,500,000 Muslims live in Bosnia—and only 500 to 1,000 Evangelicals. Reaching the disabled with the good news was not going to be easy.

We jump-started our visit with an official reception. As I greeted our guests and gave a message from the Gospel of Mark, I scanned the faces of those gathered—dignitaries from the Bosnian government, UN officials, and the US Ambassador and his wife. Sprinkled here and there were blind people, men and women in wheelchairs, Gypsies, Muslims, and missionaries. I sensed invisible walls dividing the rich and poor, the able-bodied and disabled, the Muslim, Croat, and Serb. Would this group of people be willing to help us reach the war-injured?

We drove to a hospital in Tuzla. Doctors and nurses—most of them Muslim—were skeptical at first, but they quickly warmed to us. We sipped strong Turkish coffee, discussed rehabilitation methods, laughed over the tactics of politicians, and shared common problems. Finally, they let us talk with disabled men and women in the hospital. When we departed, the doctors asked if we could return with wheelchairs. We gave each other knowing smiles. Walls of hostility were beginning to come down.

Even for me. It happened as I talked with Dario, the young Bosnian-Croat soldier who was assigned as our driver. As we drove through the ravaged countryside, past bomb-blasted villages, I gently probed him with questions.

I learned that he had served as a commander of a small unit during the war. For three years, his was a world of killing and carnage. As I put his story together with news reports, I sensed a growing distaste. My imagination put pictures to his words, and I discovered an unwanted wall beginning to rise. *How could this man have done those unspeakable things?*

Unspeakable, they were. I realized that as I listened to Dario's slow and halting speech. The horrors of the war had blocked his ability to speak clearly. His stuttering qualified him as one of those "disabled from the war." Softly, Dario described the land mines exploding at his feet by day . . . and in his head by night.

As we traveled day after day Dario continued to share bits and pieces of his story. The more he unfolded his heart, the more mine broke for him. Walls shattered. Prejudice disappeared. This was one disabled person in Bosnia who was reaching me!

On the last day as we drove to the airport in Sarajevo, he mustered strength to bring resolution to his tortured story. After we unloaded baggage and hugged goodbye, he wedged a letter in the side of my wheelchair. "Read this later, if you like," he said with a slight smile.

On the plane, miles above and beyond the hills of Bosnia, I unfolded his note:

*"I asked a German missionary who visited me and my mother if it is possible that God can forgive even so big sins like mine. He*

*answered to me that Jesus pays some 2,000 years ago ALL the sins from this world. Later that night I fall upon my knees and started to pray, crying and begging from God to forgive me and change my life. During that night I had hard nightmares. When I wake up next morning, I felt some very strange deep peace and joy inside me. It was nice sunny morning. I could hear birds singing. I wanted to pray more and to share that joy of Jesus with others."*

I leaned my head against the window of the plane. Dario's story symbolizes the only solution for rich and poor, able-bodied and disabled, brown-skinned and white, Muslim, Croat, Kosovar, and Serb: "For [Christ] himself is our peace. . . and has destroyed the barrier, the dividing wall of hostility . . . " (Eph. 2:14).

As I look back on Bosnia I'm amazed at how far hope and grace, prayer and good will, smiles and Christian encouragement can take you. They can vault you over a wall of hostility. They can, in fact, bring it down.

# HOLINESS...

# WHERE IT'S

# NEEDED MOST

# A PROMPTING FROM THE SPIRIT

**R**ush from work. Meet Judy at *Hamburger Hamlet*. Scarf down Chicken Caesar. Pay bill, exit restaurant. Put down lift and wheel into van. Oh yes, stop and pray with Judy before heading in different directions. After our "Amen," she headed for her car. While I waited for my van to warm up, I exhaled, attempting to slow my heart down from the fast-paced day. I was heading to my church to speak to our women's group.

As I pulled out of the parking space, I noticed a woman wearing a baseball cap leaving the restaurant. *I wonder who she is? That baseball cap . . . her scraggly hair.* Suddenly, I sensed a powerful urge to ask her to come hear me speak. *Yes, she must come. She needs to hear what I have to say.*

"This is ridiculous," I said out loud, alone in my van. Cars were backing up behind me. *Should I follow through on the impulse?* "What am I supposed to do, God? Roll down my window, yell for her to come over here and say, 'Hey, I think you ought to follow me to church!' That's ridiculous!"

I honked at Judy. She jumped out of her car and ran over to my window. I told her about the strange prompting. She glanced at the woman on the sidewalk, and then at the line of waiting cars. "You're blocking traffic, Joni, and you'll be late for your meeting."

All the way to church I berated myself for not inviting the woman with the baseball cap to come to church. "Lord," I prayed out loud, "next time I won't flinch. I'll follow through. I'll listen to your prompting!" Ten minutes later, as I

was pulling into the church parking lot, I was surprised to see Judy in my rear-view mirror. "You're not going to believe what happened," she said, as I spotted a van pull up behind her.

It seemed that after I left the *Hamburger Hamlet*, the woman in the baseball cap approached Judy and asked who I was. This was too weird for my friend. "Joni almost invited you to come hear her speak. Would you like to go? I'll show you the way."

There in the church parking lot I heard her story. "Earlier, my husband and I were at the UCLA cancer clinic and we stopped to eat on our way home." Her voice cracked; her husband squeezed her shoulder. Joyce—that was her name—continued. "I've had breast cancer for four years and two hours ago I learned that the cancer is now in my brain. It's inoperable. You looked so . . . happy. I don't know what to do . . . where to turn. And so, we're here."

My mouth dropped open. Suddenly I understood the scraggly hair under the baseball cap—chemotherapy. I also understood why the Holy Spirit had urged me to drop everything and invite her, a complete stranger, to come hear me speak.

That night, as Joyce and her husband sat in the front row, I talked about heaven and hope, grace and the gospel of Christ. The two strangers had an opportunity to bow their heads and pray to accept Jesus as their Savior. I shudder to think the opportunity was almost lost—because I let embarrassment

dissuade me . . . allowed pressure to fluster me . . . let awkwardness override the Spirit's prompting.

I wonder how many of us second-guess a prompting and ignore the Spirit's leading. That night I learned that *every urge to do good, every prompting to share the gospel is a prompting from God.* We need not second-guess. Second Corinthians 6:2 pushes us into action: "I tell you, now is the time of God's favor, now is the day of salvation."

This week you'll hear God's still, small voice whisper, "Say something to her . . . invite him . . . make that call . . . apologize." You'll be tempted to brush it off—but don't.
Seize the moment! Today is the day of salvation!

The prompting may never pass your way again. Neither might that person. Ever.

# JESUS SAVES!

ometimes the holiness can't stay hidden, and when that happens, it can be odd. Take last week in the terminal of Chicago's O'Hare Airport. Judy and Francie, my traveling companions, and I had bounded off the plane, charged up for several speaking engagements. Our friends from the Chicago office were as pumped as we were. They grabbed our hand luggage and together we nearly ran down the corridor toward baggage claim.

Somewhere after Gate B7, the corridor opened up into a high-ceilinged hall decked with twinkling white lights and flags of the nations. Down through brilliantly colored flags we walked, laughing and talking—a bunch of girls out to change the world. Looking up, the symbolism in those world flags wasn't lost on me. I wheeled ahead of the others and broke out singing, "We have heard the joyful sound—Jesus saves! Jesus saves!"

Judy and Francie chimed in, " . . . spread the tidings all around—Jesus saves! Jesus saves!" A couple of guys in the bar looked up. Men in business suits rushed by and grinned. Our voices rose in a crescendo with the last stanza, "Tis our Lord's command—Jesus saves! Jesus saves!"

It's not the kind of thing I do all the time. Just some of the time. If not in an airport terminal, then on a city sidewalk, or in a hotel lobby or an elevator. (Singing softly to myself is the kind of thing I can get away with. People see me in this wheelchair and almost expect me to be odd!)

That's what Anika thought. She was the shuttle bus driver in Germany who drove us from the Munich airport to our hotel. As we pulled away from the curbside, I said, "Anika, we're going to pray here in the back seat, but you're driving, so don't close your eyes!" The look she gave us in the rear view mirror said it all: *You people are odd.* She had us pegged. We were wonderful examples of 1 Peter 2:9, ". . . a peculiar people; that ye should show forth the praises of Him who hath called you out of darkness into His marvelous light" (KJV).

> Clap your hands, all you nations; shout to God with cries of joy.
>
> **PSALM 47:1**

But it's the odd things that stick in people's minds—and sometimes in their hearts. The next morning when Anika took us back to the airport, she sang softly along with us. She also thanked us after we prayed for her and her family. When we said goodbye, she commented with wet eyes, "I like you people . . . there's something about you that makes me happy. I wish I could go with you."

"You can," I said. "One of these days we're going to lift off. And we'll go higher than any airplane could ever take us! Let Christ take your hand and you'll go with us." Anika smiled. We were one more stepping stone in her life's journey which, I'm convinced, will land her in heaven.

When we're gripped by the fact that God lives inside us, pulse-pumping joy splits the seams of our soul and we can't help but act a little foolish. We shine rays of hope, share snippets of songs, snatches of prayer, and mustard-seed encouragement—and end up changing the world. A smile here, a "God bless you" there. We don't have the luxury of

85

*Holiness...When It's Needed Most*

sitting down and explaining the Basic Doctrines of Faith, but we can say, "Jesus saves!" And God can take those words, songs, and smiles and call people "out of darkness and into His marvelous light."

Every once in awhile, it pays to be downright peculiar. To the world it looks odd—but at least they're looking!

# YE RANSOMED SINNERS, HEAR

Ye ransomed sinners hear,
The pris'ners of the Lord;
And wait till Christ appear
According to His Word.
Rejoice in hope; rejoice with me.
Rejoice in hope; rejoice with me.
We shall from all our sins be free.

In God we put our trust:
If we our sins confess,
Faithful He is, and just,
From all unrighteousness
To cleanse us all, both you and me;
To cleanse us all, both you and me.
We shall from all our sins be free.

Surely in us the hope
Of glory shall appear;
Sinners, your heads lift up
And see redemption near.
Again I say: rejoice with me.
Again I say: rejoice with me.
We shall from all our sins be free.

Lyrics: Charles Wesley, 1742
Music: Lewis Edson, 1782

# A TIME IS COMING

y *God!*" exclaimed the boutique owner, a tall, blonde woman with a German accent, "It would look absolutely great on you!" She held up the jacket on its hanger, twirling it so I could see the back.

"Oh, do you know Him, too?" I asked, matching her energy with a big smile.

"Who?" she wrinkled her forehead.

"God. You mentioned Him. The way you said His name, I thought you might know Him."

"Me? Nah!" she scoffed. "I did that whole God thing many years ago. I don't need Him. I have myself."

That did it. As she rang up the sale, I squeezed in as much testimony as I could. "Oh, do you follow Jesus?" she wanted to know. "He was handsome and quite the revolutionary." She laughed.

"I don't know about His looks," I replied, "but I know He revolutionized my life." The woman—I learned her name was Anushka—eyed my wheelchair. I breathed a sigh of relief. Once again, my chair was underneath to help back up my words. By the time I wheeled out the door with my purchase, Anushka still wasn't convinced. But she did promise to read the *Joni* book if I got her a copy in German.

As I drove away, I remembered an odd little verse I had read earlier in the day. Jesus said, *"Do not be amazed at this, for a time is coming when all who are in their graves will hear his voice and come out—those who have done good will rise to live, and those who have done evil will rise to be condemned"* (John 5:28-29).

You're like me. You meet people like Anushka in your community every day. Trouble is, we never look—I mean, look deeply—at a run-of-the-mill shopkeeper and picture that person rising out of a grave, either to live or to be condemned.

Maybe it's because we can't imagine Jesus as judge, as anything other than tender and compassionate. Perhaps we can't fathom a voice so loud, so thunderous that it will wake the dead. We can't envision people actually rising from their graves. More horrifying, we are stymied at the thought of our neighbors, co-workers, or relatives rising only to be condemned. *Lord, do you mean my third grade teacher? The women who run the day-care center where I take my child? My mailman? My housekeeper?*

> *A holy life is not an ascetic, or gloomy, or solitary life, but a life regulated by divine truth and faithful in Christian duty.*
> **TYRON EDWARDS**

Let Jesus answer: *"He who does not honor the Son does not honor the Father, who sent him. By myself I can do nothing; I judge only as I hear, and my judgment is just, for I seek not to please myself but him who sent me"* (John 5:23, 30).

If people don't know Jesus, they don't know the Father.

I'm praying Anushka will. When my friend took the book to her last evening, she sniffed, tossed it aside, and said, "Maybe, if I have time, I'll read it." Then my friend told her to open it up. She saw her name and smiled. He explained, "Joni wrote it with her mouth." Her eyes widened. *"This,"* she said, smoothing the cover, "I will read."

One day Jesus will come to judge the living and the dead. The dead, we can't do anything about. The living, we can.

# THE TITANIC

**E**ven after it received eleven Academy Awards, I refused to see it. But my birthday was last week and guess what—someone gave me a video of *The Titanic*. So three nights ago, I had Ken pop the cassette into the recorder.

The costumes were resplendent with rich colors and textures. I loved the mahogany staircases, the china and silver, and the violin music. I admired the leading lady, a young woman whose creamy complexion, thick auburn hair, and stately posture cast her as a true Golden Girl. That is, until she hooked up with the leading man, a cocky, cute Tom Sawyer-type. They couldn't throw off their Victorian morals fast enough. They were a couple of wild kids from Van Nuys after a few beers. At that point, I turned it off.

I picked up the story the next night. As the ship steamed west, the sailors in the crow's nest failed to see the mountain of ice dead ahead. The pilot swung his wheel left, but the huge ship couldn't respond in time. The bowels of the ship rumbled and groaned, chandeliers rattled and champagne glasses tinkled. The iceberg had left a gash. The ocean began its slow and sure claim on the *Titanic*. Within hours, it would sink.

I was captivated by peoples' reaction. With a shortage of lifeboats, men panicked, cutting life preservers off weaker victims. Resigned to the inevitable, gentlemen poured brandy and toasted their fate. Second-class passengers never had a chance —the stairwells leading to the upper decks were locked. Mothers huddled in corners, wrapping their arms around their children. The bow of the ship went under. They were going down!

The movie was a powerful metaphor of a frightening reality. This tiny planet has been given a mortal blow, a gash in its side. Rebellion against God has set it on a crash course with hell, and whether we like it or not, it's going down . . . and dragging a lot of people with it.

Some refuse to believe it. Surely if we hate suffering, God must hate it worse and could never have founded an institution as horrible as hell. But the same Jesus who gave heaven a five-star rating also described an otherworldly chamber of horrors. "*[Hell] has long been prepared; it has been made ready . . . it's fire pit has been made deep and wide . . . the breath of the* Lord, *like a stream of burning sulphur, sets it ablaze*" (Isa. 30:33).

Stop and listen. Do you feel the rattling? The down-deep rumbling of something gone haywire? Had the Bible not told us otherwise, we might think this life was the only life there is. We'd continue to arrange our days as though rearranging deck chairs on the *Titanic*. We'd clink our brandy glasses and toast our fate, as though we were only facing a soul-sleep—a dull, gray existence without God, who, as a matter of fact, was a bit of a bore on Earth anyway.

Don't misunderstand. God didn't make hell for people. Jesus said it was *"prepared for the devil and his angels"* (Matt. 25:41). It's *unnatural* for humans to be there—as unnatural as turning our backs on a Creator who loves us. As unseemly as shrugging off the Father's kind arm while we caress Eden's serpent, coiled around our hearts.

No. God takes no joy in anyone heading for eternal misery. And His Son is the lifeboat—big enough and wide enough to rescue all of the perishing.

# RESCUE THE PERISHING

Rescue the perishing,
Care for the dying,
Snatch them in pity from sin
    and the grave;
Weep o'er the erring one,
Lift up the fallen,
Tell them of Jesus the mighty
    to save.

Chorus:
Rescue the perishing,
Care for the dying;
Jesus is merciful,
Jesus will save.

Down in the human heart,
Crushed by the tempter,
Feelings lie buried that grace can
    restore;
Touched by a loving heart,
Wakened by kindness,
Chords that are broken will vibrate
    once more.

Lyrics: Fanny J. Crosby
Music: William H. Doane

> *The greatest miracle that God can do today is to take an unholy man out of an unholy world, and make that man holy and put him back into that unholy world and keep him holy in it.*
> **LEONARD RAVENHILL**

## "PRAY FOR THE LADY!"

t was our first vacation in ten years. A Caribbean cruise through the islands. A chance for Ken and me to carve out a week for ourselves, away from the madding crowd, the pressures and demands.

We leaned over the railing of the huge ship and watched the passengers wind their way off the gangplank, through a check point, and down the narrow streets of the Jamaican village to the marketplace five blocks away. "Ready?" he asked, "Let's go!"

Decked out in flashy tourist garb, we made our way through lines of hawkers and taxi cab drivers, all wanting to "show the lady the lovely sights." We headed down the street on the right-hand side where most of the other tourists were walking.

> *It is not the man who has too little, but the man who craves more, who is poor.*
>
> **LUCIUS SENECA (4 BC - AD 65)**

I looked to the other side of the street and noticed a few beggars. *Hmmm . . . maybe the cruise line doesn't allow them to bother people on this side of the street.* Then I spotted a young Jamaican woman in colorful island dress sitting in a wheelchair next to a table of seashell necklaces. Ken and I grinned and said simultaneously, "We don't belong on this side of the street . . . we belong over there."

We crossed the street to chat with this woman and many other disabled people who lined the left side of the street. We meandered along, shaking hands, purchasing trinkets, and commenting on the beautifully hewn wooden crutch a Jamaican man was leaning on.

"Did you notice something?" Ken asked. "All those disabled people were amazed that you are a quadriplegic. They obviously don't see many people as paralyzed as you."

I looked around at the shabby homes lining the streets. "Well, maybe people like me don't survive here." It was a sobering thought.

While Ken popped into a store near the marketplace, I sat in the shade of a colonnade, greeting a few passengers I recognized from the ship. While resting, I noticed a happy looking Jamaican man seated at the corner of the colonnade. He was a one-man band, strumming a banjo while pumping drums and a horn with his good foot. I noticed his other leg was amputated. His music was lively and upbeat, so I wheeled through the small group of tourists to get closer.

His black face was scrubby with white whiskers, and his smile revealed several spaces and gold teeth. When he noticed me bob my head to the rhythm, he picked up a pair of maracas and offered, "Here, lady, come join me . . . play these!"

I smiled shyly and shook my head, "No." But when he saw my smile, he hobbled over and tried to place the maracas in my hand. That's when he drew back, stunned. He realized that not only were my legs paralyzed, my hands were too. His smile turned to dismay and he cried to those gathered, "Oh, pray for the lady! Please pray for the lady!"

The group didn't know how to react. Ken arrived on the scene and together we tried to allay everyone's concerns, especially the Jamaican man. "It's okay, really," I assured him. "I'm happy because of Jesus!" at which point he pressed his hands together and lowered his head as if to show me he would pray.

That night back in the ship's dining room, surrounded by chandeliers and silver, china and linen, I stared into the candle at our table and murmured, "What an honor." A poor man considered me poorer than himself. A disabled man considered my disability a thing to be pitied. I had received charity from a toothless old Jamaican with one leg—and couldn't have been given a greater tribute.

It's something to strive for. A life goal: to be the recipient of grace . . . to be less than the least . . . to receive the prayers of one who deserves it more—to be like Christ.

# HOLINESS...

# AND HUMILITY

# SHAME ON ME

I know that lady has her facts all wrong," I muttered. "Either that, or she has a hidden agenda."

We were behind a closed door in the corner of the restroom, so I felt free to ramble on to my friend as she helped me. I should have kept my opinions to myself. After all, it *was* a public place. And—yikes—the woman with whom I had disagreed, unbeknownst to me, was standing beyond the door by the wash basin!

When I exited the stall, I came face-to-face with her. Thankfully, her face was lit up with laughter. "Gotcha!" she said good-naturedly. "I'm assuming you were about to come back to the table to tell me your opinion, right?"

I was red as a watermelon. "Right," I said, relieved. But was I ashamed!

And rightly so. I had just displayed an inflated idea of my own importance . . . a pompous know-it-all attitude. Most of all, I blushed deep red because of my shame in misrepresenting my Lord. I knew I had tarnished the name of Christ.

Shame can be one of God's best tools in refining us. It says in Psalm 97:7, *"All who worship images are put to shame. . . ."* Usually, a verse like that makes us think of wooden figurines with fat lips and bloated bellies—something you'd see on display in the British Natural History Museum. But Psalm 97 isn't out of date. Image worship is still in vogue, and idols still put us to shame. When does it happen? Whenever we *feel* ashamed.

Think about a time when you were ashamed of yourself. Perhaps you were sitting, sophisticated and nicely dressed, with a new friend over coffee. As the conversation flowed, you felt witty and interesting. Your new friend was fascinated with you. You felt charming. Why, you were as pleased as punch with yourself. But then it happened. You knocked your cup and coffee spilled all over you. Your friend winced . . . onlookers turned their heads. Instead of laughing it off, you felt stupid and silly, embarrassed and ashamed.

> *It might be well if we stopped using the terms* victory *and* defeat *to describe our progress in holiness. Rather we should use the terms* obedience *and* disobedience.
>
> **JERRY BRIDGES**

This is where Psalm 97:7 comes in, because through shame God exposes the things we idolize. The conversation was flowing . . . you felt witty and charming. What idol did the feeling of embarrassment expose? Pride in your appearance. Smug self-confidence in conversational skills. An inflated idea of your own importance.

Remember how I blew it in the public restroom? I knew an idol had just been shoved off my shelf—the idol of self-righteousness.

Yes. Shame is a good thing. Embarrassment isn't bad. It helps us detect the idols in our life. And once our idols are exposed, we can more easily do away with them. That's why I'm continually ransacking the shelves of my heart to clear it of idols. Throwing open the closed cupboards and drawers of my mind so God can junk every graven image I keep hidden—images I didn't even know I had.

I'm relieved that God keeps exposing them. It's worth the embarrassment. It's worth the shame. It's even worth turning watermelon red!

## CAUGHT YA!

It all started with that man who looked like the mustached banker on my *Monopoly* board. Elderly and distinguished, soft-spoken and extremely successful, he was a man of integrity and well respected in the corporate world. I was honored he had taken time out of his busy schedule to visit our office. One comment he made to our staff kept echoing in my mind: "I've had to make some tough, ethical choices that weren't easy . . . but I'm glad I did. It's important to be obedient not just in big things, but in little things as well."

As I waved him goodbye from our office door and watched him walk away, I felt inspired. *Lord, I want to be that sensitive to your voice when you tell me "No, don't do this," or "Yes, head down this path." I want to be more obedient in the little, yet important things.*

That evening, at the beginning of my usual prayer time in bed, I started off thanking Jesus for the example of the businessman. I made a mental list of all the things I wanted to pray about in the next half hour or so. After I organized the list in my head, I focused my heart and embarked on what was sure to be a glorious time of praise and intercession.

Just then, Ken opened my bedroom door and asked, "Joni, remember you wanted me to remind you about that special on Genghis Khan? Well, it's started. Want me to flick on the television?"

"U-u-u-uh . . ." I stammered for a long second, kicked myself for not remembering the special, and then impulsively decided, "Yeah, thanks, turn it on." No sooner did the words come out of my mouth then I quickly breathed an apology: *Lord, let me put our prayer time on hold . . . I'll get back to praying as soon as this television program is over.*

I quieted a twinge of guilt as the opening credits appeared on the screen. At that instant, the phone rang. Ken picked it up in the other room and yelled, "It's for you. It's Bunny!"

*Bunny? Why is my prayer partner calling me now? We're not supposed to get together and pray over the phone for another couple of days!* Ken tucked the receiver between my ear and the pillow.

"What's up?"

"You tell me, darlin'," Bunny said in her southern drawl. "I was just sitting here minding my own business when the Holy Spirit said to me, 'Call Joni.' I looked at my watch, it's late here on the east coast, and I said, 'You mean now, Lord?' And He said, 'Yes, now!' So here I am calling you. I don't know why, but . . ."

I burst out laughing. "Bunny, I know *exactly* why God told you to call!" I told her about the businessman who obeyed God in the small things . . . how he had inspired me . . . how I had asked the Lord to remind me to be obedient even in little things. "And just as Genghis Kahn was about to

A man is not complete
in spiritual stature if all
his mind, heart, soul,
and strength are not
given to God.

R. J. STEWART

gallop across my
television screen,
while I sheepishly
put the Lord on hold,
you called!"

"Caught ya!"
Bunny laughed.

That was the night
the Spirit grabbed me
by the collar before
I took a step of
disobedience. *Gotcha!*
He whispered. Off
went the television.
Out of my thoughts
galloped Genghis
Kahn. Back I went
to a glorious time
of prayer.

That night before
I closed my eyes in
sleep, I whispered,
*Thanks, Lord. Grab
me by the neck anytime
You want.*

ights! . . . Camera! . . . Action!"

The two interviewers, with bronzed faces and bleached teeth, engaged the camera lens and energetically read the tele-prompter: "Good afternoon and welcome to our program. Today we are interviewing four couples affected by disability. We want you to know what it's like to live with a wheelchair in a marriage."

Ken and I looked at each other and then at the other couples. We felt like fish in a bowl. He squeezed my shoulder to relax us both. Methodically we tackled one question after the next about unmet expectations, communication, and lack of privacy.

Finally, the interviewer dropped a bomb. "I must ask all of you . . . you have sexual needs like any couple. Are your relationships fulfilling?" she said as she glanced around the table. "Joni, how about you and Ken?"

I felt steam rising. The fish bowl was getting hot. "I don't think you'd be asking such a question if we were able-bodied," I motioned to the other couples. "Society is way too absorbed in the subject of sex. It's a private matter for us, and for people out there," I said gesturing toward the camera. Ken gave my shoulder another squeeze.

Our culture is a pushover when it comes to letting passions prevail. From Washington to Wisconsin, we are being seduced. Especially Christians. But it's not at the banquet of the wicked where we stuff ourselves on evil deeds; we've become voyeurs, sampling what we've

convinced ourselves is safe, nibbling at arms-length from the table of the wicked. It's not pagans who have a problem with *"the world, the flesh, and the devil"*—it's believers.

I'm included. I may have come across a tad smug on camera, but when I wheeled off camera, it was the usual battle of prying the world's suction cups off my heart. My spiritual battleground is not over a torrid love affair or the X-rated shelves in the video store; my paralysis prevents me from reaching for common temptations. My fight of faith is played out on the field of my thoughts—what my body can't have, my mind will shift into overdrive to deliver. But daydreams and fantasies only frustrate. They only bring feelings of restlessness and dissatisfaction with the way things are.

But it's not enough to say, "I'll never think about that stuff again." The way to fight fire is with fire. To combat powerful passions, you need something far more powerful in your arsenal.

The fire of enticing thoughts *must* be fought with the fire of the pleasures God offers. If you try to fight the fire of lust with a bunch of threats and warnings alone, you're going to fail. We've got to fight the pull of earthly pleasures with the massive promise of superior happiness in God. Dr. John Piper has written superbly on this subject in *The Pleasures of God:* "We must swallow up the little flicker of lust's pleasure in the conflagration of holy satisfaction. When we make a covenant with our eyes, as Job did, our aim—get this—our aim is not merely to avoid something erotic, but to gain something excellent."

God is our aim. The fight of faith against wrong thinking is the fight to stay satisfied with God. Whether it's bad thoughts, daydreams, questionable behavior, or what transpires on a Friday night date, the fight of faith is always to stay satisfied with God. The good fight has a "good" side. All is not bad. The battle involves more than eschewing evil; it's pursuing God.

If I satisfy my thirst for joy and passion by the presence and the promises of Christ, then the power of sin in my life is broken. Dr. John Piper puts it this way, with a smile: "We do not yield to the offer of sandwich meat when we can smell the steak sizzling on the grill."

And what whets our appetite for maximum joy in the Lord? You guessed it—God's Word. The role of the Word of God is to feed faith's appetite for Jesus Christ. And in doing this, our taste buds for the deceptive savor of sin are dulled. Our hearts become weaned away from earth's pleasures—we become hungry for God.

*Holiness is not freedom from temptation, but power to overcome temptation.*

G. CAMPBELL MORGAN

## MY "SPECIAL" PEN

P eople say the dumbest things to me," complained the woman with multiple sclerosis. "They think if my legs are paralyzed, my brain must be, too. I don't know why the onus should be on me to correct the ignorant thinking of others."

It was an understandable comment. It was also a good place to air it: a workshop I was teaching with my friend,

Rana. Rana jumped in with a reply, "You need to defuse your anger, plus promote understanding. If you get the same comments time and again, why don't you memorize a short response you can readily give without getting flustered."

The group of fifty people nodded. It was a wise, practical suggestion. The woman seemed pleased. I was pleased that the workshop was going well, that we were covering ground and bringing enlightenment and awareness. I was also satisfied that people were respecting our practical insights . . . a little too pleased, if you know what I mean.

That's when my mother, who was sitting in the third row, raised her hand. *Oh good,* I thought, *Mother is participating.* Rana called on her.

> *Forget others' faults by remembering your own.*
> JOHN BUNYAN

"I want you all to know that Joni has a pat response she always uses."

Panic clutched my throat. *What is she going to say?*

Mother turned to face the crowd and announced, "Sometimes people stop Joni to ask for her autograph. It seems to happen at the oddest and most inconvenient times. Plus she has to sign with her mouth. So rather than say an outright 'No,' she comes up with, 'I'm sorry, I must sign holding my special pen between my teeth. And I don't think I have my pen with me. Bother!'"

I died a million deaths. The workshop attendees looked at each other and snickered. They read the situation well: a mother had just embarrassed her daughter in front of a lot of people. "Mother, wait a minute," I stammered to explain, "To protect my teeth, I really *do* need to use my special pen."

"Yes," she acquiesced, "but, honey, you say that even when you *do* have your pen with you." The class belly-laughed. I should have kept my mouth shut. Rana bravely picked it up from there, and the workshop continued.

It's just like a mother to do that. And it's just like God. He steps into our tightly controlled, private space, raises His hand, and says, "Pardon me, everyone. I have something to reveal about this person." He presumes on our comfort zones, tears aside curtains, throws open locked doors, and pulls the fire alarm on stuffy, sacrosanct attitudes. He oversteps our nicely organized plans and strips the veneer off our smug ways. He boldly intrudes into our sin, brashly calling it what it is and challenging us to leave it behind.

It's called *humiliation.*

It's one of the painful ways we face our sin. If we remain unaware of our sin, we cannot truly know or understand ourselves. Humiliation lands a knockout blow to self-esteem, reminding us that without Christ we are nothing. It's what I was reminded of that day in front of the workshop.

I was reminded of it again after the class was over. Someone walked up, holding one of my books, and asked for my autograph. "Oh, I'm sorry," I said, "I'm afraid I don't have my special pen with—"

I don't need my mother to humiliate me. I do it to myself.

*Holiness…and Humility*

# THE INTERROGATION

**M**y back was aching as bad as my head. The day had been a loser. I hadn't gotten a thing done. *Stupid paralysis*, I mused. *If I had my hands, I could've grabbed control of the day better.* I lobbed the thought over the net and returned another one: *How come Judy gave me that rotten look today?* I served up another one: *I wonder why I wasn't complemented on that message I gave?*

Back and forth I tossed sour thoughts in my head until the game got serious: *What's the matter with me? Why do I feel full of bitterness? I've got so much to be grateful for, and here I am stewing over nothing!* My mind grabbed the ball from my heart and began taunting: *You're nothing but a hypocrite, a fake, a liar . . . you're no good!* I answered quickly: *No, there's no*

*condemnation for those who are in Christ. I'm a child of God.*
Came back the reply: *Then think like it.*

Finally, I buckled under the assault. "Help, help, I'm falling . . . falling," I whimpered. Backward, head over heels, plunging into a dark pit. The world felt like it was caving in on top of me. "Catch me, God, please," I pleaded, like a passenger on a plane losing altitude fast.

All this while lying completely still in bed.

I was collapsing from a time of interior questioning. Suffering does this. It forces us to be utterly alone with ourselves. Once sequestered, suffering is what tests us most as persons. It examines us, sifting and asking, "Who are you, really?" In answering that question myself, I was overwhelmed by my seething resentments, greed, and an itchiness to have things my way. Usually if sin surfaces, I'm able to manipulate the circumstances so as not to appear petty or vindictive. But an aching back and pounding head will strip off that veneer.

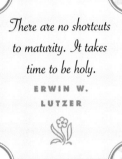

*There are no shortcuts to maturity. It takes time to be holy.*

**ERWIN W. LUTZER**

113

Suddenly, not a minute after my cry of the soul, I felt the arms of God catch me. Plop! Like falling into a feather bed— I was safe. Fear drained away. My immediate response was to cleave to Him, to cut away the sin. *Father, I was wrong. You are right. And thank heavens for this wheelchair that keeps pointing it out!*

Suffering, then, can be our friend. I need to remember that the next time my back aches and I start taking pot-shots at my paralysis. I'm too often like the thick-headed sheep who follows his dark thoughts into a darker forest. It takes the bite and bark of my paralysis, like a sheepdog snapping

at my heels, to warn me of the danger—the vices and resentments—and to herd me into the Shepherd's arms. Suffering goes below the surface, sandblasting us to the core. It brings us into a new relationship with ourselves. It also brings us into a new relationship with God. When pain and problems press us up against a holy God, guess what goes first? You've got it. The selfishness that pain unmasks. The pride and pettiness that problems reveal.

The beauty of being stripped down to the basics is that God can then fill us up with Himself. It's not just that sin is removed, the saint is built up: "Christ in you, the hope of glory." Think of the Father's joy when He sees Christ in you. Nothing pleases Him more. When the soul empties itself of pride and pettiness, Christ fills it up. It's just another way of saying, "You died, and your life is now hidden with Christ in God" (Col. 3:3).

Suffering doesn't teach me about myself from a textbook, it teaches me from my heart. It will always show me what I love—either the God of all comfort or the comfort that can become my god.

# TAKE TIME TO BE HOLY

Take time to be holy,
speak oft with thy Lord;
abide in Him always,
and feed on His word.
Make friends of God's
    children,
help those who are
    weak,
forgetting in nothing
His blessing to seek.

Take time to be holy,
the world rushes on;
spend much time
    in secret
with Jesus alone
By looking to Jesus,
like Him thou shalt be;
thy friend in thy
    conduct
His likeness shall see.

Take time to be holy,
let Him be thy guide,
and run not before Him,
    whatever betide.
In joy or in sorrow,
still follow the Lord,
and, looking to Jesus,
still trust in His word.

Take time to be holy,
be calm in thy soul,
each thought and
    each motive
beneath His control.
Thus led by His Spirit
    to fountains of love,
thou soon shalt be fitted
for service above.

Lyrics:
    William D. Longstaff, 1882
Music:
    George C. Stebbins, 1890

# AN ART LESSON

O ccasionally, I like to invite friends to peek over my shoulder as I work on a painting. That usually means they have to step over piles of crumpled papers and tubes of paint on the floor. It also means my friends may learn a lesson—and not just about art.

Like this Christmas painting. It's beautiful, it's colorful, but creating it was no easy feat. I designed my painting to look like stained glass. As such, I filled the window with symbols.

The kneeling figures of the shepherd, king, and magi suggest the Child's destiny as both Great Shepherd and King of Kings. The lamp at Mary's feet tells us He is the Light of the World. Christ is also called the Rose of Sharon, so I painted a thorny bush of lavender roses cascading around Mary. A little lamb foreshadows His role as the Lamb of God.

Pulling all these symbols together was a real challenge for me. At first, nothing looked unified. Different parts of the design kept vying for attention, competing with one another. *The robe on the king looks, ugh, garish . . . the purple color is way too bright. And the coat on that lamb is too weak . . . it needs to be stronger for this part of the painting to show up. And that lamp is way too yellow. It should be more in the background.*

Nothing in the painting fit together. I couldn't even see Baby Jesus for all the clutter and confusion. All my planning, all my hard work, and what did I have? A mish-mash.

When an entire canvas is dangerously close to getting scrapped, I often throw down my brushes and talk to the

painting. "Look, all you parts, quit thinking you're more important than the rest. Nobody on my canvas is going to outshine the others, so get in line. Let's have a little cooperation here. And let's remember just who is in the center of the painting . . . okay? It's Jesus."

Talking so brashly to a painting gives me courage to re-tackle it with more forceful strokes of the brush. I'm no longer intimidated by the paint I've already laid down on

canvas. So, with my brush, I began a more courageous attempt to give the symbols their proper relationship. Every part of the painting had to complement the other . . . or this time the painting would be trashed.

I got ruthless, working fast and furiously. I kept experimenting—brightening the violets, toning down the reds, highlighting the greens and subduing the yellows until all the parts pulled together. As the artist, I had to force every area of that painting to cooperate until the colors and the composition obeyed.

> *Each of you should look not only to your own interests, but also to the interests of others. Your attitude should be the same as that of Christ Jesus.*
>
> **PHILIPPIANS 2:4-5**

When I wheeled back to take a look at the completed painting, my eye went right to Jesus! Finally!

We're like that painting, aren't we?

Sometimes we Christians vie with each other for special notice. We're all supposed to be adoring Jesus—like the figures kneeling in my painting—but we end up muddling the message. Spoiling the focus. Yet what an awesome Artist holds the brushes! God won't stand for a mish-mashed Church. He forces us to cooperate with one another, honoring here and humiliating there, showcasing the weak and casting shadows on the strong, bringing forward one, nudging back the other, pulling and pushing us into unity until all the parts obey. And what happens when we Christians finally get around to complementing each other? The message is clear, uncluttered, and anything but abstract—Jesus, and Jesus only, is the center of attention.

Voilá! It's a masterpiece!

**H**ere, try this moisturizer before you test the foundation," the saleswoman said as she slid the small jar across the glass counter. Her name was Gabriella, and her beautiful eyes and full lips matched her classy name. It was a Saturday afternoon, and soft scents of perfume, as well as soft strains from a piano, wafted through the cosmetic department.

As Gabriella adjusted the mirror for me, she commented on my smooth complexion, as well as my smile. For me, such remarks are an open door to talk about the Lord of "every good and perfect gift," including smiles, perfume, and pianos. She seemed genuinely interested.

An hour later I arrived home with my purchases, one of which was a bag containing cosmetic items. I had my friend unpack mascara . . . moisturizer . . . foundation and— "What's that?" I said as she held up a small square box. "I didn't buy anything else." Inside was a pressed-powder compact. "Where did *that* come from?"

My friend flipped open the compact, and we admired the powder and mirror. We commented on the black-lacquered finish and delicate gold edging. The velvet pouch. The satin drawstring. "Hmmm . . . not bad," she said. I watched her slip it back into the box. She didn't say anything, as if waiting for a signal from me.

"I wonder how it got in there? You know . . . ," I paused, "I'll need some more pressed-powder in a month or so." Another long pause. "Maybe the woman at the counter

119

slipped this in as a gift?" My friend frowned. She knew better. So did I, but since I had already taken one step in justifying my actions, the next came easier: "Taking this back to the mall would be such a hassle for me."

The whole thing could have been easily solved with a phone call to the cosmetic department, but I got distracted. The next day when the urge to call resurfaced, it seemed less urgent. Time became my partner in crime, and after a week the compact still sat in my bathroom. I felt guilty, but not enough to take it back. With each passing day my lack of initiative seemed less sinful than it actually was in the sight of God. I chose to believe that sin—at least in this case—wasn't quite as sinful as God says—and that I wasn't quite as bad as I, in fact, am.

> *Saying yes to God means saying no to things that offend His holiness.*
> A. MORGAN DERHAM

A few nights later, however, I stumbled across Hebrews 3:13 in my quiet time: *"Encourage one another daily . . . so that none of you may be hardened by sin's deceitfulness."* No sooner had I closed my Bible than my conversation with Gabriella about God replayed in my mind. Some witness I was! I sighed, realizing I was a casualty of sin's deceitfulness. The compact went back to the make-up counter the next day.

You may think I worried over nothing. That the whole incident was insignificant. *Why sweat the small stuff?* But listen to what Bishop J. C. Ryle once wrote about trivializing sin.

> We are too apt to forget that temptation to sin will rarely present itself in its true colors. Never when we are tempted will we hear sin say to us, "I am your deadly

enemy . . . I want to ruin your life." That's not how it works. Sin, instead, comes to us like Judas with a kiss. . . . But we cannot alter its nature and character in the sight of God.

That's what hurts the most about my sin—it grieves God. When I was muttering, trying to excuse my actions, the Spirit was trying to get through to me: *Joni, you're off course here. Really, you are . . . are you listening? Do you care that this hurts Me?* I may feel bad when I fail a saleswoman or disappoint a friend, but it really stings to cause God grief.

It also causes me grief. Every time we cover up sin, we suppress our conscience; that is, a knowledge of ourselves as God knows us. Conscience says: *I don't care if your name is Mother Theresa and you want to sell the compact and give the money to the poor. Take it back. Period.* Conscience is God's no-nonsense watchman in our soul. His spy inside our hearts. We cannot argue with our conscience—it will never change its mind. It will only become less forceful and more faint. And when it does, *we* are the ones who become damaged.

Funny how a little gold-edged compact can be a litmus test of my love for Jesus. Yet, "Of all the things that will surprise us in the resurrection morning, this, I believe will surprise us most: that we did not love Christ more before we died," wrote Ryle.

I don't know about you, but that's one surprise I want to avoid.

# HOLINESS...

# NO LONGER

# HIDDEN!

# A GLIMPSE OF GLORY

I look for God in lots of places. Especially when I'm on the road. I look for Him when a flight is canceled or when a gate agent gives me a hard time about the batteries on my wheelchair. I look for God on empty streets in dark cities or in stuffy hotel rooms. I wait for His blessing over a late-night dinner of cold turkey sandwiches. Long trips on the road make me long for Him.

It's easy to see His glory in warm and inviting settings such as churches or conferences; but it's in those in-between places, such as car rental parking lots and airport terminals, that I long to feel His presence, sense His nearness, and see His hand at work.

It all began with a prayer from Ephesians 1:17–18. I kept asking that "the glorious Father [would give me] the Spirit of wisdom and revelation so that [I might] know him better . . . that the eyes of [my] heart [might] be enlightened." I asked to see Him in all things, and I haven't been disappointed.

Like last week. I was in the home stretch of a long journey, flying into Memphis to change planes. Busy trips like this one always get me thinking about home. Not only home here, but Home there—heaven. Thoughts of heaven filled my mind as I looked out the airplane window. Being up so high made me want to, well . . . keep going up. But we were heading down.

As our plane began its approach, I marveled at the way the lowering sun reflected off of everything wet and metallic—streams looked like silver ribbons, car windows

flashed like golden shields, and puddles looked like shiny pennies. I leaned against the window and peered ahead to see a cemetery coming up on the left side. I noticed there were no granite headstones; only brass plates marking each grave. I wasn't prepared for what happened next.

As we flew over, suddenly the sun exploded off the tops of hundreds of different brass markers in a quick-fire succession of sparkling light—bam! bam! bam! As the plane tilted, the graves, here and there, flashed as though someone were tossing fire crackers over the cemetery. I gasped and squinted against the dazzling light. Each grave ignited like diamonds detonating. In an instant, it was over. Our plane touched safely down. It had happened so fast, as if in the twinkling of an eye. Stunned, I turned to my friend sitting across the aisle and breathed, "You'll never believe what I just saw!"

The metaphor wasn't lost on me. I'd been looking out the window, looking for God . . . dreaming about heaven . . . wondering when, oh when, I might be called Home. The Lord answered and joined my thoughts, opening the eyes of my heart to gain a glimpse of glory. I got a bird's-eye view of 1 Corinthians 15:51-52 when *"we will not all sleep, but we will all be changed—in a flash, in the twinkling of an eye, at the last trumpet. For the trumpet will sound, the dead will be raised imperishable, and we will be changed."*

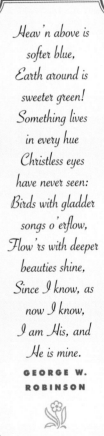

*Heav'n above is softer blue,
Earth around is sweeter green!
Something lives in every hue
Christless eyes have never seen:
Birds with gladder songs o'erflow,
Flow'rs with deeper beauties shine,
Since I know, as now I know,
I am His, and He is mine.*

**GEORGE W. ROBINSON**

Some would shake their heads and insist that all I saw was the sun reflecting at a forty-five-degree angle into my eyes. Others, less cynical, would smile and say I merely saw a beautiful display of God's handiwork.

I'm convinced it was more. It was holiness in a hidden place.

God is always revealing Himself to us through His Word and through the works of His hands. He's an intentional God, brimming over with purpose, infusing meaning into everything around us. But we need to open "the eyes of our heart" before we can see; and that, my friend, begins with a prayer from Ephesians 1:17-18.

God has sprinkled earth with hints and omens of His presence and purpose, whether in parking lots, airport terminals, or cemeteries. He's always foreshadowing His Story's ending. He once died to show it to us—you can read about it in the Bible and you can see it every day all around you. Just ask Him to open the eyes of your heart.

# HOLY, HOLY, HOLY

Holy, holy, holy!
Lord God Almighty!
Early in the morning
Our song shall rise to Thee;
Holy, holy, holy!
Merciful and Mighty!
God in three Persons, Blessed Trinity!

Holy, holy, holy!
All the saints adore Thee,
Casting down their golden crowns
Around the glassy sea;
Cherubim and seraphim
Falling down before Thee,
Which wert, and art, and evermore shalt be.

Holy, holy, holy!
Tho' the darkness hide Thee,
Tho' the eye of sinful man
Thy glory may not see;
Only Thou art holy;
There is none beside Thee
Perfect in pow'r, in love and purity.

Lyrics: Reginald Heber
Music: John B. Dykes

# BACK TO THE FUTURE

'm a home movie fan. There's nothing like a family get-together where you take out the old 1960 Super-Eight movie projector and thread it with a couple of reels of memories. It happened during a recent visit with my family when Ken and I were back in Maryland for the holidays. My cousin Eddie came over to the farmhouse with his old eight-millimeter projector, set it up and announced, "You guys are not going to believe your eyes!"

Eddie dimmed the lights, flicked on the projector, and I witnessed something I haven't experienced in thirty years. Larger-than-life on the living room wall, I saw myself at the age of fifteen. I wheeled closer to the images. It was me—same basic hair style and color, same smile as I have now—but my head was attached to a walking body . . . my body!

I was wearing a sweatshirt and jeans and holding onto the reins of my horse, Tumbleweed, while Eddie sat atop the

saddle. (He was only twelve or thirteen). Watching myself lead Eddie around the barn corral, I noticed my hands. They were holding reins, patting my horse's neck, and straightening Eddie's foot in the stirrup. I observed how my knees bent when I kneeled to pick up something in the dirt. My moccasins were old and unraveling at the seams. It gave me goose bumps to think that I haven't worn out a pair of shoes in three decades. "If only I had known then that my accident . . ." my voice trailed off.

Ken was the one who was really amazed. At least I have solid memories of what it was like to be on my feet. But Ken has never seen me that way. He's only known me in my wheelchair.

Later on he asked what was going through my head as I watched myself walk. I thought for a moment and commented, "There was a time I would have sighed, 'Aww, that's the way it used to be. I wish I could go back to that.' But now, thirty years later and almost as many years sinking my heart and head into the Word of God, I can say, 'Oh, wow, that's the way it will soon be. Heaven is coming, and I can look forward to having a body that works. And I'll do so much more than walk!'" I was so excited to know that, in the long run, I haven't lost anything—I *will* walk again.

The way I look at it, there is less distance between me and the future than me and the past, when I was on my feet. I'm closer to this side of gaining my new heavenly body than to the other side of losing my old earthly body. I have come to the place of living out Philippians 3:12, *"I press on to take hold of that for which Christ Jesus took hold of me."*

The past is the past. And the future is so much more interesting to think about, to look forward to, to dwell on.

Friend, what are you dwelling on today? The loss of something or someone in your past? Have you lost your health, your stamina? Twenty-twenty vision or good hearing? Have you lost a loved one? Do the memories still hurt?

Stop for a moment and let those memories catapult you into the future. Let your groaning be not for "what once was," but for "what will soon be!" Romans 8:23 says, *"We ourselves, who have the first-fruits of the Spirit, groan inwardly as we wait eagerly for our adoption as sons, the redemption of our bodies. For in this hope we were saved."* You have *everything* to look forward to!

To "wait eagerly" is to enjoy a happy expectation that this life (and its painful memories) is not the only life. At the resurrection—the redemption of our bodies—we'll receive back all that we've lost, and so much more. So much, that it's not worth comparing with those home-movie memories of pleasant days gone by. Your past life may have been lived in small-framed eight-millimeter style, but the future will be spread out like an IMAX movie in Technicolor and Dolby Stereo Surround-Sound. Every day lived is a day closer to that.

So the next time you find yourself sighing and longing for the past, stop and count the years. You just might be closer to the future than you think.

> *Set your mind on things above, not on earthly things.*
> **COLOSSIANS 3:2**

# PETS IN PARADISE?

always thought I responded well to criticism. That is until my book *Heaven . . . Your Real Home* went to press. I received more critical letters over one paragraph on page fifty-five than all totaled for anything I'd ever written. I penned it innocently enough: "[Animals] in heaven? Yes. I think animals are some of God's best and most avant-garde ideas; why would He throw out His greatest creative achievements? I'm not talking about my pet schnauzer, Scrappy, dying and going to heaven—Ecclesiastes 3:21 puts the brakes on that idea. I'm talking about new animals fit for a new order of things."

No pets in heaven? Them's fightin' words.

I didn't think so when I wrote them. I'm an animal lover from way back. Growing up, my bedroom shelves were stacked with books from the *Black Stallion, Lassie,* and *Brighty of the Grand Canyon* series. Being a farm girl, I loved 4H Club. I happily fed pigs, mucked stalls, curried horses, mixed formula for the calves, and slung sacks of oats—all for the love of animals.

So when I wrote *Heaven,* I happily pushed the envelope of Isaiah 11:6-7, *"The wolf will live with the lamb, the leopard will lie down with the goat, the calf and the lion and the yearling together; and a little child will lead them. The cow will feed with the bear, their young will lie down together, and the lion will eat straw like the ox."* From that we can extrapolate that if wolves and lambs are in heaven, as well as goats, cows, and bears (the apostle John saw saints galloping on white horses), then

surely there are pandas and pigs, as well as swans and schnauzers. I have no idea how they will fit, but I'm certain they will populate part of the new heavens and new earth—it wouldn't be "earth" without animals.

But not Scrappy. Not our pet cats or ponies that died.

That's when the barrage of letters came. "How could you say that?!" and "Heaven wouldn't be worth going to without Buffy!" and "You don't know my dog. He *definitely* has a soul." These people didn't understand my heart. Nor my affection for pets.

They should have been there when, as a child, I was galloping my horse Thunder across the field. She was a huge Appaloosa, and when her hoof went into a groundhog hole she fell with a thud. Thankfully, I was thrown clear, but that didn't help my bruised bottom. I wailed, rubbing the tears from my eyes. Thunder stood up, shook off the dirt, and trotted back toward me. She stopped and stood squarely over my small frame. I grabbed one of her legs and cried against her. When my father cantered up, he was amazed. Thunder was standing guard, head held high, ears up, nostrils flared— she was protecting me. She was the picture of nobility and maternal

care. If *"Every good and perfect gift comes down from above . . . from the Father of lights"*—and it does—then animals, too, reflect faithfulness, courage, love, and devotion. Pets are gifts, and they come from the Father of lights. Little wonder I didn't respond well to the tone of those critical letters!

So I took a closer look at Ecclesiastes 3:21, *"Who knows if the spirit of man rises upward and if the spirit of the animal goes down into the earth?"* Some translations state it as a fact. Others, like this verse, phrase it as a question. The truth is, we don't know.

Yet lately, as I've sunk my heart deeper into the Word, I've been wondering . . .

If God brings our pets back to life, it wouldn't surprise me. It would be just like Him. It would be totally in keeping with His generous character, a sort of "Oh, why not?!" happy-spirited benevolence. Exorbitant. Excessive. Extravagant in grace after grace. Of all the dazzling discoveries and ecstatic pleasures heaven will hold for us, the potential of seeing Scrappy would be pure whimsy—utterly, joyfully, surprisingly superfluous. It's not that animals have souls or that God owes Scrappy anything, but that heaven is going to be a place that will refract and reflect in as many ways as possible the goodness and joy of our great God, who delights in lavishing love on His children.

So will pets be in heaven? Who knows?! If Thunder or Scrappy are, it won't have anything to do with their merit—it will have everything to do with God and His magnificence.

# JUSTIFIED FOR EVERMORE

...The Lord wiped every tear away, and turned
To see his bride. Her heart had yearned
Four thousand years for this: His face
Shone like the sun, and every trace
Of wrath was gone.  And in her bliss
She heard the Master say "Watch this:
Come forth, all goodness from the ground,
Come forth, and let the earth redound with joy."
And as he spoke, the throne
Of God came down to earth and shone
Like golden crystal full of light,
And banished, once for all, the night.
And from the throne a stream began
To flow and laugh, and as it ran,
It made a river and a lake,
And everywhere it flowed, a wake
Of grass broke on the banks and spread
Like resurrection from the dead.

And in the twinkling of an eye
The saints descended from the sky.

And as I knelt beside the brook
To drink eternal life, I took
A glance across the golden grass,
And saw my dog, old Blackie, fast
As she could come. She leaped the stream—
Almost—and what a happy gleam
Was in her eye. I knelt to drink,
And knew that I was on the brink
Of endless joy.  And everywhere

I turned I saw a wonder there.
A big man running on the lawn:
That's old John Younge with both legs on.
The blind can see a bird on wing,
The dumb can lift their voice and sing.
The diabetic eats at will,
The coronary runs uphill.

The lame can walk, the deaf can hear,
The cancer-ridden bone is clear.
Arthritic joints are lithe and free,
And every pain has ceased to be.
And every sorrow deep within,
And every trace of lingering sin
Is gone. And all that's left is joy
And endless ages to employ
The mind and heart, and understand,
And love the sovereign Lord who planned
That it should take eternity
To lavish all his grace on me.

O, God of wonder, God of might,
Grant us some elevated sight,
Of endless days. And let us see
The joy of what is yet to be.
And may your future make us free,
And guard us by the hope that we,
Through grace on lands that you restore,
Are justified for evermore.

—Dr. John Piper

(*Future Grace*, Multnomah Publishing, Sisters, Oregon, 1995,
used by permission.)

# BACK IN THE SADDLE AGAIN

I wheeled down the cancer ward of St. Agnes hospital and turned into the room of Mr. Cauthorne. He lay thin and frail under a smooth white sheet, his handsome face gaunt and ghostly pale. I was shocked. Doubly so because I had always known him as the owner of the big estate across the river from our farm, the epitome of the gentleman-farmer standing on the porch of his white-columned mansion, riding crop in one hand, fox hound by his side.

Mr. Cauthorne stretched his hand in my direction and smiled through the pain. Our eyes dampened. I knew he wasn't looking at me in my wheelchair—in his mind, he was waving to me from his porch as I galloped up the dirt road

past his property. And I wasn't looking at him on his deathbed—our thoroughbreds were cantering together across fields and fences, our eyes damp from the brisk November wind as we pursued the fox.

It was Thanksgiving Day of 1963. I was fourteen years old, living on a farm in Maryland, and Mr. Cauthorne had invited me to go on a fox hunt. He thought I'd enjoy taking part in an old-timed Maryland tradition.

"Me? You want . . . *me* to ride with *you* on the heels of the hounds?" So early on Thanksgiving morning, after I had wrapped my horse's shins and braided his mane, my dad helped me trailer over to the Howard County Hunt Club. We parked our van, and I unloaded my horse, giving him a palm full of oats for being good in the trailer. Within minutes the cinch was tightened on my saddle, and I mounted my thoroughbred, gathering the reins in my hands.

I looked around to locate Mr. Cauthorne, and spotted him by the red barn, sitting atop Pepper Pot, his well-seasoned thoroughbred. He had on his red coat and black cap. Hounds circled around Pepper's legs. Dogs barked, horses whinnied, and matrons from the hunt club greeted everyone with cups of hot cider. I breathed in the wet aroma of dry hay and horses. Someone tested a bugle, and the dogs grew more restless.

Finally, the master of the hounds sounded the horn! Horses' hooves clattered on the cobblestones, and when we

> *Whatever is true, whatever is noble, whatever is right, whatever is pure, whatever is lovely, whatever is admirable —if anything is excellent or praiseworthy—think about such things.*
> **PHILIPPIANS 4:8**

hit soft dirt we broke into a canter. I reined in line behind Mr. Cauthorne and observed how he graciously deferred to the hunt master. I made certain to do the same. We crossed a stream and rode into the first field, where I spurred my horse into a slow gallop. I can still feel my hands holding the reins, my knees squeezing the saddle, the wind in my face as we raced across shaven cornfields, sailing over five-foot walls and wooden fences, the barking of the dogs and the blowing of the bugles.

We never caught that fox. But the thrill of the hunt was less in capturing a fox and more in capturing the joy and excitement of being part of a real Thanksgiving Day tradition. It made turkey dinner back at the Howard County Hunt Club . . . and it made my thanks to God all the more deep and personal.

"Do you remember that day?" I asked the feeble man before me who had been my riding partner that robust afternoon.

"That turkey dinner sure tasted good," he said weakly with a smile. He turned his head on the pillow as if to follow the memory a little further. I felt sad that disease, death, and disability could rob us of so much. *But not for long,* I thought.

I then presented Mr. Cauthorne with a copy of *The Living Bible.* We had never talked much about our faith, and I was delighted that he received the gift so warmly. Our conversation easily turned to spiritual things. Had he made peace with God? Was he ready to meet Jesus? Would he like me to pray with him?

Mr. Cauthorne has long since passed away. I think about him every once in awhile when I miss the feel of leather reins, or the burn in my muscles from sitting a saddle all day. I haven't ridden a horse in over thirty years, and the only leather I lean against now is the padding of my wheelchair. No cinches around saddles, only cinches around my middle to help me breathe better. The clip-clopping of hooves has been replaced by the click-clacking of gears and wheel-bearings.

But that's okay. I'll ride in heaven.

Alongside Mr. Cauthorne.

# MEMORIES OF HEAVEN

**E**arly one summer morning, my sister Jay and I drove down to the little Maryland farming community of Sykesville to visit Grandma Clark. She wasn't really our grandmother. She and Jay had become friends at the tiny stone church on the hill, and we had been invited to her big farmhouse for tea. I wheeled into the kitchen and was greeted by the delicious aroma of a freshly baked cake. Grandma had placed crisp white linen on a table by an open window. A breeze lifted the lace curtains and wafted in the scent of roses.

As Jay and I sipped tea from delicate cups, my eyes followed Grandma Clark. She leaned back, smoothed the tablecloth with her hand, and spoke of heaven in grand and wistful terms.

A gust of wind suddenly whipped the curtains, tossing her gray hair. She held up her hand, smiling and squinting against the breeze. Whoosh!—it eddied around the table, dizzying and lifting our spirits. The moment was delightfully strange. But as quickly as it came, it vanished, settling us back down and becoming timeless, leaving in its wake, peace and joy. I can still taste the cakes and the tea, smell the spring flowers, and see dapples of sunlight on linen.

Moments like these become instantly nostalgic, reminding us of some other time or place. We say the same of childhood memories: Lazy, late afternoons licking popsicles on a back step, listening to a lawnmower up the street, and feeling a breeze cool our brow. Or running out the screen door after dinner to collect fireflies. Or hugging our knees by a campfire,

watching the sparks fly upward, becoming stars. If we could be transported back, we'd discover that even as children we felt the same nostalgia, the "remembering" of another time or place.

It's a yearning to pass through and reach the other side, as C. S. Lewis said. These moments—whether having tea on a spring afternoon or licking popsicles and feeling safe—are whispering, "One day you'll bathe in peace like this . . . satisfaction will shower you . . . this joy will last forever." This is what we feel as children. It's another hint of heaven, like choosing the happiest point in your life and having time stand still.

*They were longing for a better country—a heavenly one.*

**HEBREWS 11:15**

In the light of my depraved appetites, I can barely imagine ecstasy going on forever. It's always something I want to grasp, but can't. I hear inklings in Dvorak's *New World Symphony*. I glimpse it in the soft gaze of someone I love. I smell it in the air at the ocean when the sky is gray and violent in the distance. I felt it once when I was nine years old, holding onto the guardrail by the Grand Canyon because if I let go, I was certain I would fly away across the wide expanse.

If these are mere omens, what will the real thing be like?

What's more, the pleasure and the joy will continue to increase in heaven. The unfolding of the story of redemption will have us taking one gasp after another, our joy and amazement ever increasing.

And it can start now. Make a memory today. It'll be a memory of heaven. A touch of holiness in a hidden place.

143

# JESUS THE VERY THOUGHT OF THEE

Jesus, the very thought of Thee
With sweetness fills my breast;
But sweeter far Thy face to see
And in Thy presence rest.

No voice can sing, no heart can frame,
Nor can the memory find
A sweeter sound than Thy blest name,
O Savior of mankind.

O hope of every contrite heart,
O joy of all the meek,
To those who fall, how kind Thou art!
How good to those who seek!

But what to those who find? Ah, this
No tongue or pen can show;
The love of Jesus, what it is
None but His loved ones know.

Jesus, our only joy be Thou,
As Thou our prize wilt be;
Jesus, be Thou our glory now
And thru eternity.

Attributed to Bernard of Clairvaux, translated by Edward Caswall

For a complete list of other books written by Joni Eareckson Tada or for more information about her Christmas and greeting cards, which she paints by mouth, contact the website of JAF Ministries at:

**jafministries.com**

Or you can write Joni at:

JAF Ministries
PO Box 3333
Agoura Hills, CA
91301
USA

JAF Ministries (Joni and Friends) reflects the vision of its founder and president, as Joni and the team seek to communicate the gospel and equip Christ-honoring churches worldwide to evangelize and disciple families affected by disability. If you would like to learn how you can partner in this effort to reach people with disabilities in your community with God's love, write JAF Ministries today.

S